DON'T DIE
ON THIRD

JAMES W. KRAMER

BROADMAN PRESS
NASHVILLE, TENNESSEE

Printed in the United States of America
3.5AP493

Dedicated to My Daughter
MIRIAM N. KRAMER

CONTENTS

PREFACE

This is a new printing of a volume which appeared some twelve years ago. The author, whom we never met, is remembered by many of our readers as a dynamic evangelist of the Billy Sunday type, whose sermons stirred the thousands throughout the land. Homiletically, these messages fail to make the grade; in expression and style, they are unlike any that we have printed— form is sacrificed in the interest of clearness, and it is difficult to read this language, some of which has not found room in the dictionaries, without getting the author's meaning; in doctrine, every sermon is based solidly on the Scriptures and is therefore sound.

Friends of this popular evangelist who were blessed by his ministry believe that this volume has a message for our day. It is definitely different; maybe we need something to jar us out of our complacency.

JOHN L. HILL

FOREWORD

At the earnest request of scores all over America for copies of certain sermons, after serious consideration I now put them in book form.

Due credit is here given to all who by suggestion or written word helped in the construction of these messages.

May these sermons continue to win souls for the Master and build up the Christian faith in the hearts and lives of all believers.

JAMES W. KRAMER

DON'T DIE ON THIRD

Not far from the kingdom.—MARK 12:34.

No game was ever won at third base. Thousands are
ready with their cheers at the home plate for the fellow
who hikes, slides, and scores. It is not the man who aims
all the time but the fellow who pulls the trigger and fires.
Do not wait for the iron to get hot—strike and make it
hot. One has aptly said, "Quit your trying—do." The
world wants results, not excuses. Our unction must function, our ship must come in, our pictures must live, and
our claims and promises must materialize. This world will
not tolerate a dead one, nor one whose shibboleth is, "I'm
going to." Unless we hustle, someone now hanging around
will take our job. The only man who ever succeeded was
the man who could not wait. If there be no opportunity,
make one. Loafing, grandstand plays, waiting for four
balls, handing out promises galore, and, above all, blam-
ing the umpire never get a fellow off third base. The man
on third must have but one thought—*score.* Freeze to
third and back to the minors you'll go, and all earth's
umpires will yell, "You're out!"

*I have known of many ministers to die on third base
because no effort was made to score.* Excellent, gifted,
faithful men! They were never known to make a bonehead
play, a wild pitch, be caught napping at first, or ever
become rattled; but they had the "Charley horse" and no
Bone-Setter Reese could adjust their troubles. They had
the "Charley horse," not in their legs, arms, or wrists,
but in the most fatal of all places—the heart. Their religion had never converted them from angels into men.
The office is nothing, the man everything. Pilate said,

"Behold the man!" God did his best when he made a man.
A great soul once said, "Get your man and all is got."
I had rather be a man than an angel. Angels are just
the vassals of heaven; they can't help being good. It's
a great prayer when you ask God to make you human.
They said of Christ, "What manner of man is this?"

*I have known of churches to die on third, making no
effort to score.* Waiting for something to happen: waiting
for the preacher, for the evangelist, for the revival to
knock a home run. They are waiting for a passed ball,
a balk, a wild throw on the part of others to reach the
home plate. Too many have the slogan, "A little more
slumber," or "Watch and wait." Some churches are
waiting for better times; waiting for the members to get
rich; waiting for the ship to come in. Oh, the churches
and colleges that are waiting for wealthy men to die and
endow them!

Sometimes it seems that all America is camped on third
waiting for Uncle Sam to support them. Many think
taxation, bonus, the dole are far better than God's plan,
"By the sweat of thy brow." All are waiting for tomorrow. If you are a failure today, the chances are that
you will be a failure tomorrow. The same waters that
flow here will flow there. You will find nothing in tomorrow that is not in today. *Tomorrow*—tomorrow—
tomorrow—where are you? There is no tomorrow. It is
today or never.

There are four classes of people at a baseball game.
These people usually cause a man to die on third or get off
third. To what class do you belong?

FIRST. *There are the kickers or knockers.* No place on
earth is "knocking" more prevalent than at a ball game.
There are those who knock their team, their town, their
boss, their job, and even their church. "Kickers do not
work, and workers do not kick." No finer motto than this,

"Pull for your town, or pull out." Pull for your boss, your job, your church, or pull out. Pull for America, or pull out. The cowboy poet expresses it in these words:

"Seems like we ought not to keep our praises for the
        grave,
For they do not encourage, bless, help, or save.
Better speak the word of cheer for a fellow while he's
        here;
Never keep your hammer out for a fellow when he's hang-
        ing about."

SECOND. *Then there are the quitters.* If all the world loves a lover, then all the world despises a quitter—the one who can't stand the gaff, the one who cracks under the strain, shows the yellow streak, deserts in the day of battle. It is not the one-night-standers but those who are loyal, the folks who stay hitched and put, that count. Some go down with every gust of wind. They are crusaders for a cause today that they will renounce tomorrow. I may not like my governor, but I'm not going to move out of the state. I may not like my President, but I'm not going to leave America. It's my America, right or wrong. It's my church, right or wrong. It's my family, right or wrong. What an ending was Paul's—"I have fought the good fight, I have kept the faith, I have finished my course."

THIRD. *The next class of people always found at a ball game are the bench warmers.* They are the wallflowers, the century plants, sculptured figures, or spiritual hookworms. Like Bob Fitzsimmons said, "They are where they ain't." They don't knock, they don't cheer. They are religious standpatters and reactionaries. Their favorite hymn is "I Shall Not Be Moved." They just sit and set and set and sit. You can't thaw them out, you can't freeze them out, and you can't fire them out.

The church must be more than a spiritual hotel serving two meals on Sunday, an excursion train to glory, or a saint's rest. The church should be a great, humming plant of machinery producing life and human character. The church must be God's great marching army going forth into the night of sin and bringing the wanderers back home. Heaven is not a place of spiritual indolence; and neither should the church "psalm" itself away. We should fire the bench warmers up or out. Unless the church undertakes this, it will face the undertaker. No wonder the Book of inspiration declares, "I would that thou wert cold or hot. So then because thou art lukewarm, . . . I will spue thee out of my mouth."

The class that never fails to get a man off third is the rooters. Birds sing sweeter, flowers bloom more beautifully, and waters are fresher because of the rooters. They give poise, poetry, and symmetry to all living. They keep humanity out of the asylum. Hub Palen never created a greater slogan than "The world's best 'ism' is optimism." Frank Stanton never wrote a more beautiful verse than,

> "This world that we're a-livin in
> 　Is mighty hard to beat;
> You get a thorn with every rose,
> 　But ain't the roses sweet."

I crave no higher honor than to be an apostle of good cheer to my fellow men. Humanity needs a boost, not a kick. I never see a man down and out, even in the ditch, but what I think of the heights from which he fell. Men may have devils in them, but they also have angels. There is gospel in a handshake, a kind word, or a smile, and a soul is worth it. I crave no higher joy than to have my friends say when I have passed on, "He was good to me."

Nothing in the universe is so sad as to see a man die on third. To see a team go to pieces in the ninth; to see a pitcher blow up in the last inning; to see a ship sail over all seas and sink within sight of the Golden Gate; to see a high school boy fail on examination day; to see a life collapse with the dew of the morning upon its brow; to have a husband and wife sue for a divorce after celebrating their golden wedding anniversary; to see a father rush across the continent to see his dying boy and have death beat him in the race; to see a man pay all his debts and obligations save those due the Lord God.

Moral man, camped on third base, you have merely crowned self, not Christ. You can't patch up your life; you must crown Jesus; and the only place that can be done is at the home plate. A man's batting and fielding average is as he ties onto Jesus Christ. Though his footsteps glitter with gold, he is a dismal failure if he is not yoked up with Christ.

Husband, a wife is waiting for you at the home plate. She does not want your money, your presents, or the material things in life half as much as she wants the family circle complete; to have you pull with her. In many homes a husband swears and a wife prays.

A mother is waiting at the home plate. Her one uncreasing prayer is "God save my child." Many a man, by his life, is helping to nail the lid on his mother's coffin. It's a positive fact that scores of mothers' lives could be prolonged if they could hear the news, "My child has been saved." Cruel the nature, stony the heart, and black the life that would not do it! What a wretch!

A child is waiting for you at the home plate. Many a child is out of the church because father is not in the church. A boy said to me once, "If my Dad can be so kind and good, so true and clean, and not be a member

of the church, why should I be?" In the judgment many a
boy will say, "I never heard my father pray." A man
should be a Christian for his child's sake if for no other
reason. If there be a place in hell hotter than any other
place, it will be for the father who will not give his own
flesh and blood the proper example. I had rather you spit
in my face, shoot me dead in my tracks than to have my
child say, "Dad, you did not do your best for me." He
shall not say it.

My friend, a Saviour is waiting for you at the home
plate. How long he has waited! Out in the long hours of
the day, out in the long silence of the night, he has waited.
You have treated no other friend as you have treated
him. Your life has been a series of intentions, resolutions,
broken vows and promises; yet, still he waits. His love,
care, devotion, and passion have never cooled or been
off duty. He has never given up. He still cries: "Let's
pull together," "Let me share your sorrow," "Let me bear
your burdens," "Let me enrich your life." Every step
from the manger to the cross was a step for you. Why wait
until the last game is played, the last ball pitched, the
ninth inning is over, to reach the home plate? All your
loved ones, the angels, the Holy Spirit, heaven, and the
Master stand at the home plate crying, "Take a chance;
run, fly, score!" God forbid that you should ever hear
the great umpire Time say, "Three strikes; you out!"

One of the finest classics of baseball is a story told of
the death of a great baseball manager in California. So
full of pathos and God were the dying words of that great
player. They would be my message to every high school
student, to every soul climbing up the hill of time, to
every father and mother building God's greatest temple
on earth, the American home. As this famous ball player
lay propped up in bed, about to breathe his last breath,
with a smile on his face, the warrior of a thousand games

said, "Boys, I have played my last game, I have just signed up with the all-star team above. Get on that team; she's a winner!"

I had rather fail with Christ than win with others.

He was world most unccempl failm

IF I HAD A MILLION

A cup of cold water.—MATTHEW 10:42.

If you had a million and I had a million, we would doubtless do our best to get another million. We can do proportionately with the one dollar what we would do with the million; with the one talent what we would do with ten. The Word of God proves it: "Thou hast been faithful over a few things, I will make thee ruler over many things." We want to do the spectacular, to play to the galleries, to shine over a wide expanse of territory rather than focus the fires of life in one God-given direction. All service for God is extraordinary. After all, who can say what is great and what is small? Sometimes what we call great God calls failure; and what we call failure God calls success. God does not weigh and measure as man does. Man judges by the outside, God by the inside. They called Herod "a god," but the worms devoured him. They said Calvary was a failure, but all Christendom sings of that failure:

"In the cross of Christ I glory,
    Towering o'er the wrecks of time;
All the light of sacred story
    Gathers round its head sublime."

"Great" people discourage me and bore me. I had rather know God's average man and woman. I had rather trust the smallest star that twinkles in the Milky Way than all the dazzling comets that ever flashed across the sky. I had rather trust the base hitters of the kingdom than all the swinging home run hitters of the theological world. Who can say which is the greater—the sermon of Peter on Pentecost or the prayer of the little child, "Now I lay me down to sleep"? Who does the greater service—he who guides a million souls to the shrine of truth or the mother who keeps fond vigil over her sleeping child? Who was the greater—Herod in his golden palace at Tiberias or Lazarus in his rags? Who is the greater—he who plants a hill of potatoes or he who plants a nation? Only eternity will reveal the good of a cup of cold water given in his name.

I want to show you that every soul has in his possession, unchallenged, that which is worth more than a million to the nation, to the home, to the church, to God, and to his fellow man. See how rich you really are!

FIRST. *How About Time?* How much will you take for a few years or hours of your life? Men fight the greatest battles to live; and they would rather live in poverty than die in luxury. Yet thousands are crying, "What shall I do with my time?" Thousands talk about "passing time away" or "killing time."

Time is the greatest gold mine in the universe, and every minute and second is a nugget of gold. God asks only two material things of us: one-tenth of our money and one-seventh of our time; and up to this hour some of us have robbed God of both.

Time for the dance, the club, bridge, the lodge, amusements of all kinds, but no time for prayer, the Bible, and sacred things. Did you know that many Christians give God only one hour for worship out of seven days? For pleasure, society, clubs, and politics they give many hours a week. What a world we would have if all Christians would devote just one hour a day to God! We haven't a million, but we have the time. The busy people are the ones who do things. The indolent, the drones, always arrive an hour or a day too late.

At the close of one of my meetings, a poor woman came up to me, placed her love offering in my hand, and said, "Here is five dollars. If I had five thousand, I could never repay you for what you have done for my family." One day I called on her husband and talked and prayed with him. I won him for Christ and a sober life. I gave him just ten minutes of my time.

Time! What a gold mine! Quit squandering time on self, chasing butterflies, and blowing bubbles. Life is more than a picnic, a house of fun, a theater of dissolving views, and a meaningless jamboree. The other fellow needs you, and you need him. God needs you, and only your dissatisfied life tells you how you need God.

You will have to give him some time before the curtain falls. Is there a more wretched thought than that of having the memory haunt us throughout eternity—"I helped no one, I blessed no one, I saved no one"?

SECOND. *How About Your Influence?* Isn't that worth a million? It has been said, "Everybody is somebody's hero." The greatest thought that ever entered my mind is my personal responsibility to God and others. I cannot escape it. What I am today may cause thousands tomorrow to thank God that I ever lived or may cause thousands to curse my memory. Sin may send me to hell, but how about the influence of that sin on unborn thousands? No other power is comparable to personal influence. Stand on the street corner, and one man is the leader. That is why we have show windows, advertising clubs, chambers of commerce, and experts. Many things I might do, but I forbear because of influence. I quit card playing, dancing, theater gadding, and smoking, not because they were against the rules of my church or would damn my soul, but because I wanted nothing in my life I had to defend. I wanted no one to say, "Physician, first try your medicine on yourself." We can't strike ten for God today and ten against him tomorrow. There is even a greater influence I would speak of than that of holding to some things and giving up others: the influence of a life that puts God first, his kingdom first, his church first.

When William Jennings Bryan arrived in Spokane, Washington, one Sunday afternoon, scores of his party met him and said, "Mr. Bryan, a great crowd of Democrats will be at the banquet to hear you speak this evening." The great Commoner turned and said: "Gentlemen, I am sorry you did not consult me. I'll not be there. I am a Sabbatarian and will worship at the Baptist church." That's what I mean by placing God first.

When Theodore Roosevelt was elected President, he was a member of the Dutch Reformed Church. It was just a little frame building with a handful of members. Four great churches in Washington said, "Free pew, Mr. President; come and worship with us." But every Sunday found the lion-hearted, wilderness-minded, seraphic soul winding his way through back streets, dark corners, common neighborhoods to worship with his brethren in a little church. That example was a sermon even the blind could read.

I heard a governor of Colorado declare at a great church gathering: "It's a great privilege to live in Denver, to be a citizen of this wonderful state, to be your governor; but I prize my membership in the Central Presbyterian Church above all."

In Cincinnati I saw twenty thousand Masons of all branches parade through the streets by Fountain Square, with twenty brass bands. As they passed the teeming thousands who lined the streets, I heard the bands play and the Masons sing, "Onward, Christian Soldiers," "How Firm a Foundation," "All Hail the Power of Jesus' Name." If Masons were not ashamed to place religion first, redeemed of God, we should not hesitate, quiver, or even stammer to say at all times, in all places, what Admiral Phillips affirmed when he saw the Spanish ships sinking, as, doffing his hat, he said, "I call upon all of you in this hour to witness the fact that I believe in God."

If you can't give anything else, give your example, your actions to every high ideal and noble endeavor. Let your shadowy life be greater than your fleshy life. God can and will forgive the last sin, but "the bird with the broken pinion will ne'er soar as high again." A thing said is a thing done. We set in motion each day influences that will never become stationary but will send forth their waves until they strike the shoreless banks of eternity.

THIRD. *How About Giving God Your Child?* Who would sell his child for a million dollars? God says to every parent, "Take this child and train it for me." He who has not tried the companionship of a little child has missed one of the richest flowers that ever bloomed in a life. Did you ever see a color like that which blooms in a child's cheek? Was there ever a sparkle like that of a child's eye? Was music ever as sweet as a child's voice?

Spurgeon said, "I have had to turn out hundreds of church members, but never excluded a child member." No, I am not in favor of a religious stampede for children. We should never herd them into the church; yet we should never prevent them.

Who ever made a father or mother the pope of the child's soul? Can't you write on a clean sheet of paper better than you can on a spotted sheet? Can't you play on a full-stringed instrument better than on that of one string?

Can't God take these young lives with all their innocence and cause the unruffled stream of his love and purity to flow through their souls? Must a child take a degree in sin and be covered with the ravages of it before that child is a subject of divine grace? Any child who knows enough to go to school and learn reading, writing, and arithmetic knows enough to learn of Jesus. Any child who knows enough to take dancing lessons or witness some undesirable picture show and understand it, knows enough to follow Christ.

It seems to me we are cowards. We are demanding more of our children than we demand of ourselves. If God will be as hard on us as we are on our children at times, then the curtain will forever fall on us. The grandest sight I ever saw was my own blue-eyed, golden-haired darling kneeling at her mother's knee repeating her first little prayer, "Now I lay me down to sleep." I doubt not that at that scene the angels hushed the flutter of their wings and the songsters of the skies momentarily lost their chords; while over highlands of glory and the floral hills of heaven God's celestial choir sang, "A little child shall lead them."

FOURTH. *How About a Little Service for Christ and Others?* A kind word, a handshake, a little push, even a cup of water—all have their place in the kingdom. God's great law of goodness is not absorption but diffusion. Over the door of the church, home, and every temple of freedom should be found these words, "I am here to serve." God appreciates even small service. This world needs a little bit of love—a little bit of you. You will never save the world with motions, resolutions, preambles, or scraps of paper. Humanity needs Y-O-U and Y-O-U-R-S.

In my church in Los Angeles I had an outstanding usher. I never heard him pray in public, never heard him make a speech, but he was the finest usher in America. One night at a roll call meeting twenty-two men and nineteen women stood up and said, "It was the handshake of Robert Roseberry, at the front door, that won me for Central Baptist Church."

Do you remember the day when someone came into your life, when you faced a great trial? Maybe there wasn't a word spoken, but the way that person took you by the hand made you his friend forever.

One day, while attending Louisville Seminary, I was discouraged—at the end of my row, all doors closed, did not know which way to turn, dead broke. I said: "God Almighty, I am a red-blooded man. If you want me to preach the gospel, I must not be humiliated, embarrassed; the money must come." I packed my grip, ready to leave for South Carolina. I walked down New York Hall, and whom should I meet but the greatest of all preachers, John A. Broadus. When I passed him, he held out his hand and said, "Hello, Jim!" I didn't have any idea that he knew my name. He said, "Jim, you are having a hard time; it's a hard pull, but stick to it like a man; I am for you." Did I stay there? I would have stayed there if I had been compelled to wade through ten thousand hells after the great Broadus had said, "I am for you." Yes—humanity does not care for your pictures, your promises, your rainbows—it wants Y-O-U.

I am more concerned about seeing God in my fellow man on the streets than I am about seeing him on his throne. I am more anxious to make Denver, where I live, and every city a holy city than I am to see the Holy City.

After a minister had preached on heaven, describing its beauty, a rich deacon said, "Pastor, you did not tell us where heaven is." The pastor walked down the aisle, and when they stood in the front door, he pointed to a hill and said: "Deacon, in the house on that hill is an old widow—she is lonely and hungry. Take her a basket of food, talk to her, read the Bible to her, and you will find out where heaven is." Heaven is right next door to the place where we find need, want, and duty. Christ said: "I was an hungred, and ye gave me meat: . . . thirsty, and ye gave me drink; . . . sick, and ye visited me. . . Inasmuch as ye have done it unto one of the least of these my brethren, ye have done it unto me." Even a cup of cold water in Christ's name shall not lose its reward.

If you cannot win a grown man for Christ, how about a child? If you cannot be a flaming evangel, how about being a pioneer, a forerunner, a pathfinder, a seedsower? All we are we owe to those who have blazed the trail. If you cannot preach, teach, or dogmatize someone to Christ, how about loving, living, or touching someone to the Saviour? The incense which God loves the best is not that which is burned in some golden altar, but that which wastes its perfumes over the habitations of the needy, weary, and wayworn.

Do the best you can, and God would not love you any more had you the talents of a Fulton, a Franklin, or a Morse. Give what you can—a million or a cup of cold water, a smile or a kind word, a boost or a handshake. In the day of eternal fruition all heaven will say, "The greatest gift of all because love hath done this."

THIRD AND MARKET STREETS
SAN FRANCISCO
WHAT ABOUT IT?

In the corners of the street.—Matthew 6:5.

Christ preached more sermons on the street than in the Temple. Solomon said, "Wisdom crieth . . . in the streets." We read of the prophet running "to and fro through the streets." People almost live on the streets today. Even heaven will have golden streets. God pity the church that does not advertise itself to the shepherdless multitudes in the streets. We are commanded to go out into the highways, lanes, and alleys and compel them to come into God's house.

One day I stood on the corner of Third and Market streets, San Francisco, and, not excepting State and Madison, Chicago; Seventh and Broadway, Los Angeles; Forty-Second and Broadway, New York City, I have never before seen as many people pass one corner as passed there that afternoon. I want to give you four great truths that came to me as I watched the throngs pass by.

First Truth. *A Crowd Doesn't Amount to Much, After All.* A circus, a parrot, or a fool can draw a crowd. The finer things of life are not worked out in a crowd. God's Word says, "Thou shalt not follow a multitude to do evil"; that "no king is saved by the multitude of an host." The Word says also, "Not by might, nor by power, but by my Spirit, saith the Lord." It was the crowd

[16]

that crucified Christ. God told Jonah that thousands in Nineveh did not know their right hand from their left.

As I looked across the street a policeman was arresting a man, and a crowd was there. On one corner stood a patent medicine crier, and a crowd was there. At another place was a dog fight, and a crowd was there. Yonder came Charlie Chaplin, and a crowd was there. David made a great mistake when he said, "I have a thousand warriors. Who can stay my hand?" He believed in the power of the crowd. But you can't always trust a crowd. Teeming thousands said of Herod, "He is our god"; but the worms devoured him, and soon the people had a new god. Napoleon said, "I propose and dispose, too." Yet when exiled on St. Helena, he cried out, "Alas, I have neither friend nor foe." It is said the deadly asp tickles before it stings. The world always cheers before it damns.

The greatest compliment I ever read of being paid to any man was paid to Elijah by Elisha. When God sent the fiery chariot to take him home, Elisha lifted up his hands and shouted, "My father, my father, the chariot of Israel, and the horsemen thereof." Did you ever hear of one man's flesh and blood being likened to God's fiery chariots and celestial horsemen? I can say with John Wesley: "I prefer one man, moved by a great master passion, than all the vulgar multitudes. I would rather have the prayers of one 'shut-in' than an 'all-star' team of preachers. I have never preached that one man is as good as another man. It is not God Almighty's mathematics. The difference in men may be the difference in one and ten thousand." Here is God's word for it, "One man of you shall chase a thousand," and "Two [shall] put ten thousand to flight." Lord Cornwallis, during the Revolutionary War, said of Dr. Richard Furman, then

pastor of the First Baptist Church of Charleston, South
Carolina: "I dread the prayers of Richard Furman more
than I do the entire American Army." The Belgians, in
World War I, exposed the weakness of numbers. China
has numbers, but she is the skeleton of all nations. Little
Japan once walked up and slapped the jaws of the giant,
China.

Do figures lie? Nothing lies so persistently. Let your
padded church rolls testify. Numerical strength is a boom-
erang. The church has trusted too long in the crowd. It
was when the Methodists were called "Methodists" in
sarcasm and ridicule; when the Baptists did not have an
organ in the church or hardly a D.D. in the pulpit; when
hundreds of the officers of the Salvation Army were put
in prison for preaching the gospel that they were a power
for God.

No one said much about Jesus except a few saved
Mary Magdalenes, blind beggars, and doubting Thomas-
es. Crowds and majorities cannot touch ideals. Patriotism is not defeated because it is in the minority. They
could crucify Christ but not the ideals for which he
stood.

Give me the God who heals the broken wing of a bird;
who paints the cheek of the peach and the rose; who
covers the defenseless head of his child with the shadow
of his wing; who catches the tears as they fall from our
eyes and changes them into prisms of glory through which
the soul can look and see the lights of other shores. The
majority has too often been on the side of evil. Alexander
the Great, with his army, shook the earth, but never as
Paul and Silas shook it with the gospel. Herod was no
match for Christ. Queen Mary against King Jesus made
an uneven fight. In every age God has reserved unto
himself thousands who have not bowed to Baal. One man,
with God, is a majority.

THE SECOND TRUTH that came to me as I stood on that corner was the fact that *all were in a hurry*. There is perhaps no place on earth where people walk and move faster than they do in the City of the Golden Gate. They tell us that the secret of it all is in the ozone; that it stimulates every nerve and stirs every sensation. When I observed the hurry and bustle of the crowd, the nervousness, the rapidity, with which they moved, I said, "That's one of the damning sins of America—'speeditis.'" I call it "Americanitis." "The destruction of the tower of Babel, the world's first skyscraper, was God's protest against hurry," said Dr. Jordon. I am not surprised at the conclusion of Henry Grady, the Georgia boy working on a New York newspaper, as he stood one day at Forty-second and Broadway watching the throngs rush by. He knew no one, and of course none spoke to him; and he said to himself, "I'm going back to Georgia where folks know each other and speak to each other."

I wish I could tell you what I saw in twenty minutes on Broadway one day. A sixteen-story building fell and nineteen lives were lost in the wreck. In a few minutes the fire laddies dashed around the corner and another life was ended. Startled and frightened, I hurried toward my hotel, and four big policemen darted by carrying a man on their shoulders. He had shot his brains out in a cheap rooming house. I said to myself, "What is a human being in New York City? No more than a worm. If I were to die, who would shed a tear—who would care?" It seems, in this feverish age, life is nothing but a lottery, or a blind man's bluff. We are going to hell at the rate of a mile a minute. Everywhere you hear the cry, "Off with the brakes." The world has forgotten the message of the Man who said, "Let us withdraw, let's rest and tarry, take stock and ponder, meditate and pray."

Passing through a city of a million people one day, I noticed hundreds of business mottoes significant of this racing age. Here are some: "Quick Lunches Served Here"; "Fixed While You Wait"; "Curb Service"; "Ready-Made"; "Make It Snappy"; "Step on the Gas"; "Atta Boy, Atta Boy."

It seems nothing short of the impossible will satisfy us. We want things of the Big Bertha type. What a bore serious and sacred things are? We have not only cut the candle in two; we are burning all four ends. Too many fathers are playboys and too many mothers gadabouts. I can give you the history of many couples: Met yesterday, married today; divorced tomorrow.

Would not this be the program of many families? Monday night—auto ride; Tuesday night—bridge; Wednesday night—lodge or club; Thursday night—picture show; Friday night—dance or party; Saturday night— dinner party; Sunday night—trip or some other pleasure stunt. One round of heartaches, disappointments, and empty dissipations. Life is just a picnic, a mad rush for the land of phantasmagoria. No wonder a rich man, walking through his gilded mansion and running his hands through his hair, moaned: 'Wine, cocktails, cards, dance, society, automobiles; no God, no Christ, no home, no children, no sabbath. O God, I wish I might have been a pauper!"

We have lived so fast we have crowded Jesus Christ out of our lives. Babylon, Nineveh, and Sodom could not escape, and neither can we. Payday comes, and the paymaster—sin is never a day late. Just as rivers flow to the sea, so does the River of Sin empty into hell. The swiftest, most merciless, and certain thing is the payment of sin. The smallest star that twinkles in the Milky Way is one of God's detectives on the track of evil to punish sin. To every devotee of Bacchus, to every forgetter of

God, to every slave of appetite and passion, I would cry,
"Stop—breakers beyond."

THE THIRD TRUTH. *I Saw Hundreds of Successful
Faces That Day to One Contented, Happy Face.* Did
you ever study the man on the street? Did you ever study
the human face? It has a language of its own. One said
long ago, "Behind the face lies slumbering all the good
and evil qualities of the soul." When the natives looked
into the face of Judson, they said, "A Jesus Christ man."
One night in Chicago, Mr. Moody asked the chief usher,
"Who is that man ushering in the right aisle? I don't
like his face; get him out." It turned out to be the man
who one month later slew the President.

More have been damned by their successes than have
been damned by their poverty. What a mess Adam and
Eve made of their perfect environment! Only Christ
could stand on the pinnacle of the Temple and be tempted
of the devil as he was and not yield. If Ingersoll had
been less an orator, he would have been less a defamer.
David never forgot God until he became a king. Lot
was a godly man until he moved over into Sodom. Success has its perils. The greatest preacher, orator, per-
sonality, I ever met was a man's man; he scintillated; he
was voted the most friendly man in St. Louis at one time.
In an unguarded moment he forgot himself, because he
was addicted to a damnable habit of which he had never
broken the chains. One day I said to him, Oh, W. J., how
could you do it?" He looked at me and replied with a de-
jected grin, "Jim, the most friendly man in St. Louis!"

This world cannot satisfy—brick and mortar, flesh and
blood, only torment us in the end. The devil is bankrupt
and can't pay one cent on the dollar. Gypsy Smith never
uttered a greater truth than, "The devil is a good 'getter
in' but a mighty poor 'getter out.'" He who made more
Americans smile than any other seldom smiled. Vander-

bilt, with all his gold, yellow and hard, when dying, turned to his wife and said, "Please sing, 'Come, ye sinners, poor and needy.' " I have known human hearts to break, and bleed, and burst, even when covered with diamonds and pearls. It's the way of the cross that leads home. Can we not believe the words of England's greatest statesman, "Christ satisfies my every longing"; or, as one great American said, "My path, like the path of the just, shines brighter and brighter unto the perfect day"; or, as Paul declared, "I have learned to be content in whatsoever state I am"? That's life, not mere existence.

FOURTH TRUTH. As I saw the hundreds pass that corner, I noticed *they represented every kindred, every race, creed, color, and environment.* I could not help but exclaim, "What a melting pot America is!" Then the greatest thought that ever entered my mind came to me. It revolutionized my theology. I did not believe less but more. From that hour I saw humanity, evangelism, foreign missions, Calvary, and John 3:16 in a new light. Three passages of Scripture came to me: First, "God . . . hath made of one blood all nations of men"; second, "God is no respecter of persons"; third, "God so loved the world, that he gave his only begotten Son, that whosoever. . . ." Here is how it all came home to me. I saw two women pass that corner. One was the most beautiful my eyes had ever beheld. Grace had found an abiding place in her person. She wore enough jewels to have retired me forever. As she passed, men bowed with profound admiration and smiled.

The other woman who passed was chained to the wrist of a policeman. She was painted with the shame of hell. The same crowd, which had smiled and bowed to the other woman, hurled out their damns upon the woman of the street. But, as I stood there, I could not help asking the questions, "Which one was the fairer babe in her mother's arms?" and "Which one had heaven cared for the most?" I wondered if the heart of the rich shone as brightly as the diamonds she wore? And again the passage rang in my ears, "God is no respecter of persons." Christianity is for the other fellow. Perhaps the most dynamic message that ever came across the Atlantic was one word, the following:

SALVATION ARMY, NEW YORK CITY
Forty-fifth Anniversary
O-T-H-E-R-S
WILLIAM BOOTH

Others—that's the word back of foreign missions and Calvary. You can't crowd the other fellow out of the way because God and your better (?) self are in the way. The grace of God is not capriciously given. None can build a wall around salvation and exclusively claim God as his God.

The chief function of a new Testament church is found in our Lord's answer to John's question: "Go . . . tell John . . . the blind see, . . . the lepers are cleansed, . . . to the poor the gospel is preached." No sinner can throw himself out of God's heart any more than we can throw God out of his world. While I could sign the strongest document ever penned by man on total depravity, I still believe when God saves a man, he is worth saving. I am no worm of the dust; I am an heir of immortality. If Jesus died for me, I must have been worth dying for. Dr. Vance said, "Every man, however sinful, is a divinity in disguise, a god trailing in the dust." If every man has a devil, and he has—he also has an angel, and Christ never failed to find the angel in man.

Just as a deformed child has a larger place in mother's heart than any other, and just as she would do more for that child than for any other, so God's sinning, erring child has a large place in God's heart. If there were a soul on earth that Christ did not die to save, gladly would he come to earth and die again to save that one.

If you were to ask me upon what I bank my hope of heaven, it would not be upon the fact that I am a member of the church, nor that I was ordained to the ministry, nor upon the fact that I have won a few souls for the Master; but I would come and plant my feet upon one word in John 3:16—"Whosoever"—and I would say, "God Almighty, that means me."

"Whosoever asketh, Jesus will receive;
Whosoever thirsteth, He will relieve.
See the living waters, flowing full and free;
Blessed 'whosoever' that means me."

QUIT KICKING MY DOG AROUND

He was angry, and would not go in.—LUKE 15:28.

The prodigal represents the underdog in the fight, and the elder brother who stayed at home is the self-righteous Pharisee who kicked his brother when he was down.

How my heart goes out to the underdogs!—folks who have gone down in the fight; the ones who have never felt the footfall of luck nor tasted the spoils of victory. Thousands cannot "take it" as we say today. They can't "cut the mustard"; somebody "has their number." Millions are trying to beat their way back. No use to walk up and say, "I told you so!" when a man falls. No need to remind him it's the judgment of God upon him. The world is not looking for the preacher who will merely tell men of their sins but rather the one who will tell them how to get rid of their sins and how to find themselves. The disgrace is not to fall but to stay there. Many find life a treadmill of existence. They look into the future and see no avenue of escape, no change, no compensation, no renewal. There are four effectual ways of kicking a man when he is down.

Just Leave Him Alone. Shut yourself up to the man who needs you. Pass by on the other side of the street and simply ignore him. You haven't any time for such interruptions. Let him go to the charity agencies or soup kitchens. I know of no opposition so cruel, so merciless, so unbending, so unrelenting, and so damnable as that opposition that freezes you out by letting you alone. I prefer a good enemy any day to a bad friend.

Look at this elder brother. All the way along he had been so self-centered. Never had he put a straw in the way of his brother's leaving. Never do we read of his calling the prodigal "brother." Look at the satire and sarcasm in the words, "But as soon as this thy son [note that he didn't say 'my brother']was come," as though it reflected great dishonor upon his father for having such a disreputable son.

It seems to be the spirit of the age. Hear the cry of this selfish, pharisaical, hell-bent earth! "I must look out for number one"; "Charity begins at home"; "I'm not responsible"; "Every man for himself"; "He made his bed hard, let him lie on it"; "I've done my duty"; "He had his chance."

This is one of the sins of the church. It is not hard to get people to join the church; but they come in one door and go out the other. It's the preacher who meets them, shakes their hand, and welcomes them. We turn them loose in the churches with their graveclothes upon them, like Lazarus, and the last condition is worse than the first. I have come to the definite conclusion that the training, development—I started to say, and I will say— the organization of a soul, is all important next to the salvation of a soul. God says to every church as a raw recruit comes in, "Take this child and train him for me." To bring a new-born soul into a prayerless, Christless, passionless church is like trying to convert a lamppost into a flower.

In a large western city a Baptist preacher woke up one morning to find he owed the merchants there three hundred dollars. It was discovered that the church owed this preacher one thousand dollars back salary. He resigned, the church paid him, he paid the merchants, and had seven hundred dollars left; but it was all too late, for he had forfeited the respect of the businessmen of that city. It broke his back and his spirit, and finally he had to go to a hospital. All the time he was there, not a deacon or a member called on him—they just let him alone. In the day of judgment God will not let that church escape.

In that same western city a man high up sinned against God, society, and his family. He was a prominent member of one of the leading churches. The Masons and Rotarians appointed committees; they talked to him and his wife; he was restored to his home and family. But in that darkest hour of his life all the officials of his church did was to meet behind closed doors and kick him out. It was later proved that not one of them had ever called to talk and pray with him to help win him back.

One night in my church in California my deacons were about to exclude one hundred resident (not non-resident) members. We read their names, one by one, and it was discovered that only five out of the one hundred had ever been called on and prayed with.

I have mistreated only one soul in my life in the way of persecution, and he was a preacher. I never wrote a word against him, and I never spoke a word against him. I just let him alone; let him dig for himself. How my conscience lashed me! Finally, I made it right with that preacher, and we became undying friends. When I walk up and down the golden streets of the new Jerusalem, where he is now, how much happier I'll be to see him because I made restitution!

You can't leave the other fellow alone; you can't shut yourself up to him, because God and all heaven will not stand for it. There are too many hells in that kind of life. No sin did John the Baptist lash more than the spirit of the Pharisees—sweeping through the Temple with their costly paraphernalia; uttering their hollow shibboleths; yet not deeming God's poor worthy of a look. There is little use to preach "God is love" (and we should love one another, for true religion is love) if we hold in mortal error at arm's length from us for fear of contamination all who disagree with us and worship not at our altar. What a contradiction! what hypocrisy! We should take one another "for better or worse."

Another Way to Kick a Man Is to Criticise Him. It seems that this is not a day of "give and take" but a day of dismembering, dissecting, defamation, censure, crimination, and castigation. How do you like this rule for the tongue? Never say a word against anyone, and you will never have a thing against anyone. The very moment an evil word is spoken, you are on the defensive. One has declared, "A thing said is a thing done." The elder brother criticised his brother to the servants and to his father and said things he must have rued the rest of his days. I'd give my arm to take back some of the things I have said. Do you remember when Saul died and false friends of David came to him and virtually said: "Saul is dead, here is your chance, strike back! Think how he humiliated you and embarrassed you! Why don't you get even now?" But this great, magnanimous heart of David replied, "Is there anyone left of the house of Saul to whom I may show the spirit of kindness?" It may be manly to strike back, but it is divine to forgive. The law of revenge has always failed.

Sampson, going down the road one day, found honey in the carcass of a lion. He stopped and "washed" his hands in the honey. I wish we might bathe our eyes, mouths, tongues, and even our words in honey so that we might never let slip words that cut, and sting, and burn.

When the artist painted the picture of Alexander the Great, he painted it with his hand covering the scar as if in a salute. I wonder if we could not with the hand of love throw a veil of forgetfulness over the faults of our fellow men and even pray for them.

At the close of the Civil War, several were discussing an old dead hound. One said, "The poorest dog I ever saw"; another remarked, "Yes, not only skinny but ugly"; another said, "The meanest dog"; but finally an old Negress said, "But, white folks, dat dog has the whitest teeth I ever saw." I wonder if we were to look long and hard enough would we not be able to see some good in all. Too many still want to call "fire down from heaven" to consume those who do not adhere to their standards, but the Christ God cries out, "Other sheep have I which are not of this fold."

Another Way to Kick a Man Is to Lie About Him. Criticism usually ends in lies. The elder brother told three lies on his brother, and then lied about his own father. How low the human heart must stoop to lie about one's father! The father was shocked and merely said, "Not so, son, you are mistaken; all that I have is thine."

But we must not be too hard on the elder brother, for few can affirm today, "I am a George Washington." One says, "There are a thousand ways of telling a lie and never moving the lips." A man's entire life may be a lie. Dr. Talmage said, "The clothes you wear, your voice over the phone, your dishonest day's work, or your broken vows and promises may proclaim you to all mankind a liar." We are living in an age of prolific liars. Look at the signs in our cities: "Going Out of Business," "Must Vacate," "Selling Below Cost," "Can't Pay the Rent."

Still Another Way to Kick a Man Is to Slander Him. What a stain the elder brother tried to place upon the prodigal when he said, "Thy son who hath spent thy substance with harlots!" A slanderer is the greatest humbug I ever saw humbugging. He is in the bottomless bottom of the bottomless pit. Slander is a sugar plum to thousands. I had rather be the poorest cannibal in darkest Africa, yea, an unconscious negation, a nonentity, than a chattering, jabbering, caustic, iconoclastic, loquacious blatherskite whose foul verbosity would blacken the reputation of an angel. Many are guilty of slander, whisperings, and idle talk. Too many have "inside dope." Lincoln, Wilson, Harding, Theodore Roosevelt had mud thrown on them. All the saloons, brothels, and gambling hells have not hurt the church half as much as gossiping tongues. James was right when he said, "A gossiping tongue is the fire of hell." I am ashamed to tell you I had to break up two ladies' aid societies because some man or woman was "catching it" from 10 o'clock in the morning till four in the afternoon. I said to a man in Los Angeles one day regarding a woman, "The most beautiful creature I ever saw." He replied, "Yes, beautiful, but all men are afraid of her tongue."

Sam Jones said there were women with tongues so long they could sit in the front room and lick the skillet in the kitchen. One of these women met a member of my church in Los Angeles one day and said: "I want to tell you something you should know. Every day at 12 o'clock noon Dr. Kramer goes to a confectionery store on Broadway and chins with the cashier." The member of my church informed her that the cashier was my sister. It was the joy of my life to give my sister a few minutes of my time, but if that black tongue had had her way, where might I have been today?

We have no right to gossip or listen to it. The most yellow coward of all is the person who comes and says, "Don't bring me into this." I'll not hear anyone's charge unless he is willing to father his own statement. I believe the devil fumigates perdition every time a slanderer passes. Strive to be something higher than a grave digger, a society scavenger, a keyhole reporter, or a gutter dweller. To every gossiper, slanderer, whisperer all humanity should shout, "Take all, but leave me my good name!" What a world we would have if everyone could act like that great lord did in England. At a banquet, many were discussing the faults, habits, and shortcomings of a man. Finally one arose and said, "Your Lordship, you know him better than any of us, what have you to say?" The great man replied, "Gentlemen, all you say about this man may be true, but I know so many grand and beautiful things about him that I have forgotten all about the little things you have mentioned."

Salvation Through Jesus Is for All Classes. Could there be a better application? "Came to seek and to save that which was lost." Christianity is not only a religion for the survival of the fittest, but also the unfittest. That infidelity which denies the power of Christ to save to the uttermost is as mean as that which denies the Triune Godhead. Thank God for a Christ who felt no pollution in catching the hot tears of a woman in sin, whose ear was not ravished by the cry of blind Bartimaeus, and who felt no disgrace in the question of a dying thief!

The preacher has one big job today, and that is to make this sin-cursed world believe that God loves it. A soul who is saved by Christ must believe that One was wounded for his transgressions and bruised for his iniquities.

The sweetest message that ever fell from the galleries on high is John 3:16. In Chicago a man was on his way to the lake to end all his troubles. As he passed a mission, he heard the singing and went inside. In a great testimony meeting which followed, he stood up and said: "Men, it works; Christ saves. I was on my way to end it all and stumbled in here only to stumble into the arms of Christ." Thank God, Christianity works, and it is the only remedy ever offered for the sins of this old world!

Millions can sing:

> "E'er since, by faith, I saw the stream
> Thy flowing wounds supply,
> Redeeming love has been my theme,
> And shall be till I die."

I have had my excursions into the land of fancy, mysticism, and rationalism. I, too, have wandered off after strange gods, but from all these adventures I have returned singing,

> "Nothing in my hand I bring,
> Simply to Thy cross I cling."

THE GO-GETTER CHURCH

The gates of hell shall not prevail against it.—Matthew 16:18.

What do I mean by the "go-getter church?" I mean a church that has a punch, one that clicks, one of dynamic power, one that justifies its existence, and, in the language of the world, one that "goes to town."

In many quarters today there is a shrill whistle of antagonism against the church. Men are saying the church has outlived its usefulness, sinned away its day of grace; that it is an outworn and outgrown program. In a great eastern city twenty thousand paraded, carrying banners with flaming printed words, "Up with Christ, down with the church." In great centers of population and cosmopolitan cities, the church has packed up bags and baggage and left the downtown district; moved up on the hill and become a family church, a church of snobs, a Sunday performer. One thought in passing: the Catholic Church has never left the downtown center. The masses of people are downtown; even sin and hell reign supreme amid the bright lights.

With all our church machinery, with all our millions of members, potential influence, a minority of the underworld laughs us to scorn and defies us to enforce the law. And up to this hour they have licked us to a fare ye well. Saloons, brothels, and gambling hells open all hours of the day and night and the church of God open only two or three hours on Sunday!

Of course, hundreds of churches can't even draw a baker's dozen Sunday evening. The man of the street has no desire to go to a funeral service, sit in a frigid air plant, or take part in a pink tea affair. The church with an undertaker's sign over the door and a ghost preaching in the pulpit will never draw men unto God. Give the people real, dynamic, honest to God gospel messages and they will come. Let the First Baptist Church, Dallas, Texas, or Temple Baptist Church, Los Angeles, and others testify. Look at the proof: First Presbyterian Church, Seattle; First Baptist and Henson Memorial, Portland; First Baptist, Minneapolis; Baptist Temple, Brooklyn; Tremont Temple, Boston; First Congregational, Boston; Conwell's Temple Church in Philadelphia; Fourth Presbyterian, Chicago; Tabernacle and Druid Hills, Atlanta; Third Baptist Church, St. Louis; Bellevue, in Memphis, and hundreds of other pulpits where the gospel is being preached. Preaching the gospel and nothing else is the great magnet and drawing power. Christ said, "I, if I be lifted up from the earth, will draw all men unto me."

With the possible exception of one man, I know of no preacher who still depends upon modernism, the new social order, humanism, and educational lectures to get a night crowd but what he preaches to vacant seats. That holds good also at most morning services.

May I give you my conception of a real New Testament church? I'll give both sides, human and divine.

FIRST. *The Go-Getter Church Must Present Humanity a Workable Program.* A church must know where it is going, what it is doing, and what it is here for. Not like the drunk in San Francisco who staggered up and asked, "Can you tell me which side of the street is the other side?" The man, pointing, said, "That's the other side of the street"; and the drunken man said, "Well, that's funny, a fellow over there said this was the other side."

There is nothing men will respond to quicker than to

feel they are in the grip of a pulsating program. The church must have power or go out of business; and the sooner the better and the larger will be the dividends. Churches can't go on doing business at the same old stand, with the same old profit and loss. An undertaker had a sign over his place of business which read, "What's the use of walking around half dead when I'll bury you for fifty dollars?" God never intended for his church to be a wallflower, a century plant, a holy retreat, or a shady spot. Some churches have had their preachers feed them regularly twice on Sunday so long that they have spiritual gout and don't know it. Good workers are good eaters, and good eaters should make good workers. Nothing but a real, spiritual evangelistic program will save the church from standpatters, landmarkers, reactionaries, or filibusters. No kid-gloved, soft-pedal, milk-and-water, pink tea, pussyfooted, powder-puff effort will ever win men to God.

Do not forget this: While the gospel never changes, programs, methods, and approaches do change. The stars you see are the same stars Moses saw, but we do not look at them through the same glasses Moses used. We view them through great observatory glasses. They are the same stars, but they seem ten thousand times nearer, larger, and brighter.

The gospel never changes. We love it because it is old, and yet it is just as fresh as the sunbeam that kisses your cheek. We no more need a new gospel than a new sun to shine in the heavens; or a new mother to love us. This gospel grows fresher each day. Talk about modernism—nothing is so modern as Christ and him crucified. Christ keeps up with the procession. It's not "back to Christ" but "up to Christ."

We may cry innovations, but the church is a series of innovations. Let me prove it. The first church I was pastor of did not have a musical instrument. My deacons would rather have had rattlesnakes crawl down the aisle. In this church women were not allowed to speak or pray in public. The deacons put a padlock on their mouths. What would a prayer service be today without women? The Sunday school, the B.T.U., women's auxiliaries are all innovations. The way our denomination and mission boards are organized today would have been rank heresy fifty years ago.

Change is coming whether we want it or not. I am a believer of believers, an orthodox of the orthodox, but, if there is anything worse than heresy, it's blind orthodoxy. Many are orthodox in their heads but rotten, miserable heretics in their lives. I prefer a real good modernist any day to a corrupt fundamentalist. I believe in creeds, doctrines, and dogmas; but God never intended for creeds to be signboards, mileposts, and eternal residences. A creed must be clothed with flesh and blood; it must take the field for Christ. The church must be a great humming plant of machinery, a great gospel factory producing character and life. The church will never be worthy to be called "the Bride of Christ," never be "as terrible as an army with banners," never truly represent Christ here during his absence until it has a working program. There is no institution on earth that has a workable program like the church if only men would work it.

SECOND. *The Go-Getter Church Must Be Largely a Young People's Church.* How our hearts appreciate and go out to the men and women who, through sleet and snow, shadow and storm, amid discouragements and defeats, have held up the banners of the Lord—and sometimes without any compensation or even a word of praise! I never stand in their presence that I don't feel virtue coming out and know I am on holy ground. I would rather have their virtues than the wealth of all the seas. Without their counsel, guiding hand, and spiritual ballast, what a house built on the sands the church would be! Yet, after this tribute to the aged hands who have studied and guided the ark of the covenant, the church needs the young people on the firing line. "The old veterans," as one has said, "may be cooler under fire but, like Jim Jeffries, he can't come back."

There is a place for the boy and the girl in the church. I have never believed the drunkard in the ditch was an object lesson in temperance. I have shuddered even to hear some evangelists drag out their past lives and tell of the hells they passed through. We do not want to place a premium upon crime. There is nothing heroic in sin. When we are saved, Christ blots out even the memory of sin so we cannot remember it. I believe it is the vision of the clean, beautiful and holy that helps. Many a boy in a home today is in a worse place than if he were in prison. Many a home is not a home but a jail with the father and mother sheriffs. I don't blame some for growing up to detest the church. When I was a boy, if my mother wanted to scare me out of twenty years growth, all she had to do was to say, "Look out, Jim, a preacher (or a policeman) is coming," and I'd hit the grit every time. The church is not a fold with the goats and sheep on the inside and the lambs on the outside.

God never intended for his church to be an old maid's paradise or a bachelor's spotless apartment. If I were pastor of the greatest church on earth, I'd let the sunshine in. Suppose it did fade the carpets—carpet bills are cheaper than brothel and gambling bills. Let the walls of my church be scratched; I'd rather have the walls scratched than to have the boys' and girls' characters scratched. Give the boy and the girl a place in the church —we need their enthusiasm, faith, vision, "pep," and

sunshine. Pastors are asking, "How shall I conserve
my young people?" The church that hasn't any program
for its young people will nurse the ashes of its own
desolation.

We should solve the problem by having frequent programs (perhaps weekly) of Christian inspiration and
wholesome entertainment which will attract our young
people and draw them away from the dance halls, night
clubs, and other questionable amusements. Why tell men
of their sins and never point to a remedy? The church is
God's spiritual Annapolis and West Point. Let the
young people come in; they are safer on the inside than
on the outside. The church provides about the only moral
training thousands of children ever receive.

THIRD. *The Go-Getter Church Must Be an Inspiration-
al Church.* A man said to me, "I never go to church. I
can't stand the humdrum of the church: it is the most
juiceless, lifeless, and saddest institution I know of." I
wonder if we are responsible for that conception of Christianity? There is nothing doleful, funeral-like, or dead
about religion. Jordan is not a hard road to travel; God
is not mistreating his children. God could have made
this world without a star, a rainbow, or a flower; but God
is in love with the beautiful. A Christian can smile—and
a smile is not the badge of an unregenerate heart. One
has said, "Smiles are the fingerprints of God in the face."
I know that back of a smiling face must be a smiling
heart; and the religion of Christ puts a smile on one's
face. Christ is even called "the One Altogether Lovely,"
"the Fairest Among Ten Thousand," "the Lily of the Val-
ley," "the Rose of Sharon," and "the Bright and Morning Star." Solomon declared, "Her ways are ways of
pleasantness and all her paths are peace." David said,
"He [the Lord] hath put a new song in my mouth, even
praise unto our God."

You will never make me believe that the Christ who attended the wedding feast at Cana of Galilee, blessed little children, rode into Jerusalem amid children singing "Hosanna, . . . Blessed is he that cometh in the name of the Lord," never smiled. We read, "God shall wipe away all tears from their eyes." All the infidel books ever written since the days of Tom Paine have not hurt Christianity half so much as this long-whiskered, lumbago type of religion. The world has been living in the minor key too long. Religion to many is a strangulation instead of an inspiration. Sam Jones said, "It's biliousness instead of righteousness." I know it seems to get into some folks' windpipes and almost strangles them to death. A Christian is not a bristling porcupine but a silhouette of the skies. Away with your skull-and-crossbones, smile-if-you-dare, hark-from-the-tomb-a-doleful-sound type of religion! It is not the beautiful religion Christ brought to this sin-scarred earth.

We can be happy without being frivolous or hilarious. The one angel that will never desert a man is the smile of his mother's face.

Keep the home fires burning in your church and men on the outside will never pass your hearthstone and warm at other firesides. No service club, no lodge, no society should have more good fellowship than the church. The poet struck a popular chord when he wrote:

"It makes a man feel curious, it makes the teardrops
     start,
   An' you sort o' feel a flutter in the region of the heart;
You can't look up and meet his eyes—you don't know
     what to say,
   When his hand is on your shoulder in a friendly sort
     o' way."

The Rockies of Colorado are great, grand, colossal, and beautiful—but how cold! I meet thousands as I travel from coast to coast who, like the Rockies, are mighty men and women upon whom God has lavished his greatest genius. They dazzle me with their talents, but, like the Rockies—how cold! When I meet them I draw my wraps tighter around me; they chill me, they freeze me. Thank God that I meet thousands also who by their "happy good morning" or "God bless you" nerve me to do the impossible. When you come into their presence you feel, "it is springtime in the Rockies" and you could go out and throw the world over your shoulder for Christ.

Ophelia's quaint slate expressions still live: "What's the use of having a smile and not using it?" "Smile and make your face limber up." "Every smile you miss leaves a freckle." All should say what the king said in the darkest hour of his life to his preacher: "Thank God, it's no worse"; or what Adoniram Judson said after seven years in Burma without a single trophy for the Kingdom, "The prospects are just as bright as the promises of God."

God is not dead nor on a vacation. Things do not run riot through the soul. To all evil he has said, "Thus far shalt thou go and no farther." Somewhere there is a Waterloo for every evil. The forces of construction are greater than the forces of destruction. Beyond the Niagara of every ruin is the rainbow of promise. God still rules the world. All the forces of evil and the devils of hell, all the ravages of devastation will and must give way to the church with a happy, cheerful, triumphant, overcoming faith. The church can go into the hottest battle shouting, "If God be for us, who can be against us?" No wonder Emerson said, "Hitch your wagon to a star."

FOURTH. *The Go-Getter Church Must Be a Church With a Vision, and That Vision Must Be of a Twofold Nature.* First, that the world without Jesus Christ is lost. Stanley tells us that when he met black men in his African journeys, they never knew they were black until they beheld for the first time his face, the face of a white man. In this land of churches, colleges, and privileges, there are thousands whose footsteps glitter with gold who will never know they are sinners until they stand by Calvary and have the white life of the Son of God fall upon them. A man is not lost because he is a sinner, moral man, bad man, but because he refuses to accept the only remedy God ever provided for sin—the atoning blood of Christ. If you want to get a man near the kingdom, get him down on his knees confessing his sins. Something must happen then, and will. The issue is not on until then. The gospel leaves no hope for a man who dies in his sins.

The second aspect of that vision is that the world, with Jesus Christ, is saved. No physician or scientist is so sure of his cure as we Christians are that we have in Christ the remedy for all our ills. Other religions may save the body, the intellect, but only Christ can save the soul.

Mr. Infidel, after all your fights with God about the mistakes of Moses and his writers—how about the saved man? How about the drunkard who had his thirst quenched in the shed blood? How about the woman who beat her way back to virtue? And the one who was once lost but now is found? The saved man is the unanswerable argument of Christianity.

There are hundreds of millions now living who can shout out the divine soliloquy that Paul sang on his way to God's beautiful "Up Yonder": "This is a faithful saying, and worthy of all acceptation, that Christ Jesus came into the world to save sinners; of whom I am chief."

The Go-Getter Church Must Be a Bible Reading and Praying Church. One of our leading preachers declared,

"Just as stall-fed beef are the best beef in the world, so Bible-fed Christians are the best Christians in the world." The Bible says that the new-born soul must "live . . . by every word that proceedeth out of the mouth of God." Get people to read the Bible and accept Christ as Saviour and wars will cease, for true Christians love one another. Get the people to read the Bible and church mortgages will be burned up, for the tithes will be brought into the storehouse. Get people to read the Bible and church divisions and dissensions will heal, for the church should be a brotherhood.

The Go-Getter Church Must Be a Praying Church. You can't slander God cheaper than to put self on the throne and prayer on the shelf. You can't run a church on dry machinery or when there is ice on the trolley. We need less theology and more *"kneeology."* The world has never been afraid of a preaching church, but all hell trembles in the presence of a *praying* church.

Bishop Johnson said, "We need not high churchmen or low churchmen, but deep churchmen." The world, infidelity, and hell can shout out your preaching but not your prayers. Just hit the trail God has blazed. Give prayer a footing in your life and flashes will come from the sky, for the wires are never down up there. Play safe and have praying men and women on your side.

FIFTH. *Above All, the Go-Getter Church Must Be a Soul-Saving Church.* A church in New York once reported a three hundred thousand dollar budget raised, and yet it had only six baptisms. It cost the Lord fifty thousand to save a soul there. That is like spreading a pound of butter on a bite of bread. Many preachers in the seminary study everything save how to win a soul. There are ministers, D.D's., L.L.D's., Ph.D's., who know everything save how to give a gospel invitation. Learning and scholarship are not all. Sam Jones said, "Better know your A-B-C's in heaven than your Greek and Hebrew in hell." The church is too often like what was said of Israel, "A luxuriant vine, but fruitless." "The glory of God departed" hangs over the door of every church that wins not souls for the Master.

The only church worthy to be called "The Bride of Christ" is the soul-saving church. The finest advertising on earth is to have souls saved. Conversions not only ring the joybells in human hearts but also revive, revamp, and fire all church activities. God is always red-hot on the track of a preacher or a church that has passion for souls, and so is humanity. The world is still crying, "Uncover the cross," "Release Jesus," "We desire to see Jesus." The salvation of one soul in your city may mean more than the coming in of a new railroad, oil well, or factory.

If you want the greatest joy that ever thrilled a heart, or the greatest motive that ever fired a soul, or be able to do the most delicate and competent work, be a soul-winner. If you want a reputation that will live when the stars grow gray with age and Time's thunder shall shake the earth for the last time, win a soul for Christ.

I would rather win a soul for Christ than blow the trumpet that will wake the dead on the resurrection morn. Destroy every pulpit, burn down every church, wreck every altar and he will sit on his mediatorial throne—the Saviour of his people.

ARE YOU FROM MISSOURI?

How can these things be?—JOHN 3:9.

Nicodemus had to be shown. This is an age of signs and demonstrations. All things, however historical, traditional, or biblical, are being examined. Thank God, we have a Christianity that steps out in the open court and says, "Try me, prove me!" The Word says, "This thing was not done in a corner." Humanity must be shown, for it demands proof and not conjecture. Thomas Edison showed us what was what in the electrical world; Babe Ruth in the baseball world; Henry Ford in the automobile world. An enormous salary awaits the man who can show the other fellow "the how."

Christianity cannot be solved mathematically. It is not a Euclid's problem nor merely a hypothetical conjecture; it is a believing, working faith. Great mischief and dismay, if not fatal distrust, have come to the kingdom because so many demand that all others be saved in the same way, with the same feelings and emotions which they experienced. God will not save all by any two-by-four rule of man. All will not be smitten with blindness as was Saul of Tarsus, nor will all suffer from the lashes of conscience as Saul did, for all have not led his life. God does save instantly, miraculously, in the twinkle of an eye, but all do not enter the kingdom alike. It took Christ but a second to win Matthew, but he labored three years with another man before winning him. God forbid I should ever preach that salvation is a growth or that it comes by education or culture. There must be a time when God meets man and speaks peace to his soul, when "the burden of his heart rolls away" and he knows Christ has redeemed him; but no two persons will have the same experience. God was not in the earthquake or the fire but in the still, small voice.

Some theologians preach a series of sermons telling men what to do to be saved, but it took Paul just a few seconds: "Believe on the Lord Jesus Christ, and thou shalt be saved." Don't go to John Wesley, to John the Baptist, nor to John Calvin to find the way, but come to the New Testament. There is nothing hazy, mystical, or unfathomable there. How simple the way of Christ! He said to Zaccheus in the tree, "Come down, I want to dine with you"; and Jesus' visit resulted in his salvation. To Matthew he said, "Follow me," and immediately he left all and followed; to the woman who sinned, "Go in peace and sin no more"; to the dying thief he said, "Today shalt thou be with me in paradise," and the gates were opened; to the rich young ruler, "Pay the price." No red tape, no probation, no penance, and no graduations. What is it to be saved? I want to discuss it negatively first.

What Salvation Is Not

It is not being religious. In the darkest days of paganism men had religion. The scribes and Pharisees had a religion that shone forth like a streaming comet. Jesus refused to acknowledge their claim. The man who holds his hand up all day until it becomes rigid, or wears spikes in his shoes, or kills his own son to appease the wrath of the gods has religion, but who wants that kind? Saul of Tarsus persecuting the Christians and putting them to death, and holding the clothes of the dying Stephen, had religion, and he tells us he thought he was doing the will of God. When they burned witches at the stake, they thought they were doing the will of God. Too many have religion, but the pity of it is that religion does not have them.

It Is Not Reformation, Renovation, Nor Confirmation.
As one has said, reformation is only a patch, a reconditioning of the soul, or a spiritual manicure. May I venture this statement? I believe the majority who backslide do not backslide from regeneration but from reformation. Salvation is not a spiritual veneer, a cessation of hostilities; not a makeshift, a compromised neutrality, an emotional acquiescence, a patronizing attitude, nor even a hallelujah experience. Too many reform every New Year's Day.

It Is Not a Feeling. A man may die and go to hell and never have any feeling. There is nothing so demoralizing, so fossilizing, so paralyzing, so cauterizing, and so petrifying as feeling. If feeling like it were salvation, all jailbirds would be converted before tomorrow night. How can a man have any feeling when he disobeys Christ? Let any soul take one step toward Jesus Christ by faith and he will have feeling enough to last him a lifetime. The Bible does not say, "Feel, and be saved" but "Believe, and be saved."

It Is Not Morality. The moral man exalts self, the Christian exalts Christ. The moral man suffers from "egotitus." I have never met a moral man who failed to give this line: "I pay my debts, I'm kind, I give to the poor, I follow the Golden Rule, I don't do any harm." It's I, I, I. As one has said, "There is no I, My, or Me in the Lord's Prayer. It is "Our Father," "Our sins," "Thy kingdom," "Thy Name," and "Thy glory." Yes, a man may be memorialized, canonized, eulogized, stabilized, standardized, baptized, idolized, and even simonized, but in the day of judgment he will be surprised if his soul is not vitalized in the blood of Jesus Christ. Morals may make a beautiful lamp but a mighty poor light.

What Salvation Is

I like Paul's definition better than any other, "If any man be in Christ Jesus, he is a new creature." Nothing transitory or migratory about that! Salvation is a new order, a new life, a new vista. When the Everglades in Florida were drained, a new Miami appeared. When they killed the mosquitoes in New Orleans, a new health was ushered in. The telephone, the airplane, the radio ushered in a new order. Salvation is a new life. Paul could say, "The life I now live, I live by Christ." Salvation is not a new frame around a picture but a new picture in a frame. Salvation is not deadening the pain, treating symptoms, but a thorough cure. When a man is saved, he has a new appetite. Here is where I part with socialism—it says change a man's environment or circumstances and he will be a Christian. The gospel says, change a man's heart and he will change his own environment. Adam and Eve forgot God entirely in a perfect environment. Here is a man who would sell the shirt off his back for a drink or stick his hand in fire for cocaine. Does that man need to be put in prison or have a pair of handcuffs to keep him away from evil? No, he needs a new appetite. What that man needs is the quickening and regenerating power of God's Holy Spirit. Paul tells us a sinner is a dead man—dead in trespasses and sins. The sooner our preachers return to Christ and preach the great distinctive principle of the New Testament—regeneration—the sooner the worldly amusement question will be settled. Let any soul make a royal surrender of his life to Christ and, when puzzled, ask the question, Is this right or wrong? Like a flash the answer will come.

Salvation Means Having a New Will. I am not leading the Christian life alone. It has been tried and tested, reinforced by a new, divine Ally. No wonder Paul could say, "I can do all things through Christ which strengthen-

eth me." If I am in Christ, let the devil hurl his fiery
darts at me; they will strike the breastplate of righteousness or shield of faith and fall aimlessly to the
ground. No wonder Luther could say, "I neither can nor
will revoke anything. . . . God help me!" No wonder
John Bunyan, in jail ten years for preaching the gospel,
could say, "Turn me out and I'll preach the gospel tomorrow." No wonder Chrysostom could say, "Go tell
your Empress I fear no power but sin." A new will, a
new power, and a new working force come into a Christian's life when he is geared up to Christ.

No one knew what Peter would do when he stood before the damsel, but all the world knew what Paul would
do when he stood before the philosophers on Mars Hill,
or what Daniel would do when commanded not to pray
in his Jerusalem window. Might as well have tempted
an angel from his throne with the plaything of a child,
or have told the sun not to shine. If I am saved, I have
a new reserve and a new reinforcement.

Salvation Means a New Motive. "The love of Christ
constraineth me." That does not mean divine compul-
sion, coercion. It does not mean compel, but impel and
propel. When a man is saved, there is opened up within
him an inexhaustible fount springing up into eternal
life. It is a divine urge, something that forces the cur-
rents of his life into a new, God-given channel. No longer
is he a legal servant just following the skeleton of duty,
the dry anatomy of legality. It is a love that goes the
last mile and breaks the alabaster box of precious oint-
ment. With this new love, no longer does he go to church
because it is his duty but because of his desire to worship.
The Christian does not pray and read his Bible because
it is the conventional thing for a church member to do
but because the Bible and prayer are the Christian's
meat and because he delights to do God's will. Jesus

does not lash a man to do his duty. All Christians should be able to say, "I delight to do Thy will, O God."

Why does God demand that a man be born again? I'll answer this way: Here comes an Englishman and says, "Uncle Sam, I want to be an American." Uncle Sam will reply, "You must be born again, swear allegiance to that flag." But the Englishman says, "I am a graduate of Oxford, there is not a stain on my name, and the purest blood of England flows in my veins." Methinks I can hear Uncle Sam say, "Bosh, I do not care who you are or where you came from; if you want to be an American, be naturalized." Here comes a man to the Masonic lodge and says, "Worshipful master, I want to be a Mason." The worshipful master will say, "Kneel at that altar, swear allegiance to our tenets and principles." Imagine the candidate saying, "But, worshipful master, I am a Methodist, or a Baptist, or an Odd Fellow." The master of the lodge would probably say, "Forget it, if you want to be a Mason, take upon yourself our obligation."

If Uncle Sam and the worshipful master have a right to say these things, hasn't the God who made us ten thousand times more right to say, "Ye must be born again"? A great evangelist once declared, "If a man could go to heaven in his sins, heaven would be hell to that man." Imagine the purest woman on earth compelled to spend the rest of her life with libertines and reprobates. A sinner in heaven would be as improbable as strawberries on a snow-capped mountain, or a lamb among coyotes. You can't get sinners to church now. What would they do "in that land where congregations ne'er break up and sabbaths have no end"? Nothing that defileth or contaminates ever enters the pearly gates.

You ask, then, what can I do to be saved? Not one thing except repent of your sins and believe on Christ.

The brightest angel of God could not do a thing to earn salvation. If it could be attained, earned, or bought, heaven would have few citizens, for it would be priceless. Because of its simplicity, men reject the gospel. Millions think, as did the Philippian jailer, that they have to do something. Paul informed, said, "Man, you can't do a thing but believe on the Lord Jesus Christ, and thou shalt be saved."

The only thing a soul can do is to accept what has been done for him. We do not like the word "debt;" it is an ugly word. How happy you would be tomorrow to throw your arms around your wife and say, "I am out of debt." Talk about paying a debt to God—who could? We can't, because we are all bankrupt to begin with. We do not have to pay for it, because Christ paid that debt on the cross and canceled all sin, so that we can all sing, "Jesus paid it all, all to Him I owe." Salvation is a gift and not a thing to be merited. "The gift of God is eternal life."

While you cannot do a thing, yet, if saved, there are some things you will do. You will come clean and clear-cut to Christ. You will clean house and make restitution. Sin and righteousness cannot live together. When a man is saved, he will make the crooked thing straight, and right the wrong. He will try to obey the Commandments and all Christ's teachings.

Have you confessed him, joined the church, been baptized, partaken of the Lord's Supper, tried to win someone to Christ? "Ye are my friends, if ye do whatsoever I command you."

When you come to Christ, you must come as you are. Christ does not save good men or bad men, moral or immoral men; Christ saves sinners. It is not the humiliation of the creature that Christ demands but the humiliation of the sinner.

> "Come, ye sinners, poor and needy,
>   Weak and wounded, sick and sore;
>   Jesus ready stands to save you,
>   Full of pity, love, and pow'r."

HONEST-TO-GOD FOLKS

Thou art Peter.—MATTHEW 16:18.

If there ever was an honest-to-God man, it was Simon Peter. Yes, he had his faults, blemishes, even sins; yet Christ loved him because he saw so plainly revealed, back of the garb of the disciple, the real man that he was. God did a real piece of work when he created a four-square, straight-shooting, red-blooded man. The individual that God has a hard time with is not always the immoral one or the wicked one, but the pinheaded or peanut-brained person; the one who will do things for which there has never been any justification. These little things which, like an X-ray, reveal the inside. I would rather be a man than the brightest angel of God. Angels are block systems, cash registers, having no will of their own. God is not saving the world through the perfect work of angels, but he has a wonderful way of using our blunders to advance his kingdom. Name one thing America needs more than real manhood. The late President Coolidge said, "We do not need more men but more man."

FIRST. *Honest-to-God Men.* Peter is the personification of a sincere, trustworthy, earnest, and honest man. He was open and above board in all he said and did. He was free from cunning, almanac piety, and duplicity. At least, he was no hypocrite. You saw the best and the worst in him at the same time. He was never known to doublecross a man, never turned state's evidence, never threw his team, never was a squealer, and never was a stool pigeon. If he was your friend, all knew it; and if he was your enemy, all knew it. He never ran with the hare and held the hound. If he was for you, he was for you for life, until the last dog was hung, the last man was out. You can trust a man like that as you would your own mother. Any degenerate son of Adam can stand by a man when the sweet waters flow and flowers bloom and the birds sing, but it takes a spiritual Hercules to stand by a fellow when he sails into the teeth of the wind and faces some modern Gethsemane or Golgotha.

In this day of race distinctions, foul methods, satire, whispers, and gravediggers, is there anything more beautiful for America than the flower of friendship? Friendship, the beautiful conception of heaven; and the lack of it, a bleak and dismal hell.

Our friendship, like Peter's, must be on time. When Christ needed a friend, how quick Peter was to draw his sword! When all hestitated, he went into the sepulcher. When all refused to speak, Peter cried out, "Thou art the Christ" who "hast the words of eternal life." Your brother needs you now. Ten or twenty years from now, those who need our sympathy will perhaps be beyond the vale of our help.

Bishop McIntyre tells us that one day his phone rang and a voice said, "Come quick, Bishop; she is dying." The bishop said he hurried to the home, but death had arrived first. The husband met him at the door and said, "Bishop, you are too late; she has just died. Tomorrow when you preach her funeral sermon, I want you to tell the people she was the best woman that ever lived, best pal, best sweetheart God ever gave a man." The bishop looked at him and said, "Amen, John, but why didn't you tell her that while she was alive?"

The poet wrote:

> "O friends, I pray tonight,
> Keep not your kisses for my dead, cold brow;
> The way is lonely, let me feel them now.
> Think gently of me; I am travel worn;
> My faltering feet are pierced with many a thorn.
> Forgive, O hearts estranged, forgive, I plead!
> When dreamless rest is mine I shall not need
> The tenderness for which I long tonight."

If we could take all the beautiful inscriptions chiseled in cold stone in the sleeping cemeteries of this earth and translate them into daily life, what a world we would have, what good it would do, and how heaven would be pleased!

Many have looked upon Peter's frankness as a weakness. A selfish, dishonest, hypocritical world cries out today: "Conceal!" "Dodge!" "Pussyfoot!" "Compromise!" "Let George do it!" "Look wise and say nothing!" "Trim your convictions!" "Water and weaken the Ten Commandments!" "It's not your baby!"

What do I mean by an honest-to-God man?

I mean one who is free from religious cant, piousness, and manufactured holiness. Most of us shine in borrowed plumes, especially when we are away from home. How many are willing for their breast to be made of glass so all can read? I am not what I am in the pulpit. When in a meeting preaching, I am somewhat on dress parade. I am what I am when I am shut up alone in my closet, with nothing between me and God's throne but my naked soul.

"Bobby" Burns' words, "Oh wad some Power the giftie gie us to see oursels as ithers see us!" might be changed to, "Oh, for the gift to see ourselves as we really are."

Others see the outside. They weigh us, and because they want to please us they pronounce a flattering decision.

You do not have to label a Christian. If a man is not a Christian, he does not cheat, deceive, or fool anyone but himself. If you are a Christian, the whole town knows it. Your servant knows it, your dog knows it, and all heaven and hell know it. You can't palm off Christianity on the world. All humanity can love a weak man, a sinner; but everyone has supreme contempt for a hypocrite. It must be an awful thing to be a hypocrite, for I have never heard a person say, "I am a hypocrite." The world will tolerate hypocrisy in the lodge, in politics, in business, but never in the church.

What is cant? It is the antithesis of a sincere soul. When a man sings, "I Love Thy Kingdom, Lord" and swaps the prayer meeting off for any "shindig" that comes along, that is cant. When a man prays, "Thy kingdom come," and has God's tenth in his pocket, or will not speak to his brother, that's cant. When a man prays to God on Sunday and *preys* upon his fellow man on Monday; shouts for prohibition and keeps a demijohn in his cellar; sheds an ocean of tears for the heathen across the seas and not a tear for the heathen here at home, that's cant.

Though written in cowboy vernacular; Brininstool's poem expresses our sentiment regarding the honest-to-God man:

"Oh Lord, let me be easy on the man that's down,
   Make me square and generous with all.
I'm careless, Lord, sometimes when I'm in town,
   But never let them say I'm mean and small.

Make me big and open as the plains,
   As honest as the horse between my knees,

Clean as the sun behind the rain,
  And free as the bird singing in the trees.

Won't you ride, dear Lord, beside me
  When I see the danger sign,
And through the storm and stampede guide me
  With your hand a-holdin' mine?

Let me treat my foes with kindness,
  May my hand from blood be free,
May I never thru sheer blindness
  Git the brand of Cain on me.

On the range of Glory feed me,
  Guide me over draw and swell,
And at last to heaven lead me
  Up into the Home Corral."

It takes something more than a shingle with golden lettering upon it to make a lawyer. It takes more than a sheepskin and a degree to make a professor. It takes more than a medicine case to make a doctor. It takes more than a white tie and a Prince Albert coat to make a preacher. It takes a real man. Sam Jones said we have in this country millions of ladies and gentlemen but few real men and women. Real manhood needs no crown for its brow; it has already reached the throne and been coronated.

God give us men who have joy without shouting for it and courage without whistling for it. When I die and my friends, few or many, gather around my grave, may they be able to say, "He lived a man and died a man."

SECOND. *Another Great Need Today Is the Honest-to-God Woman.* Never since the angel first spread its wings has there been a greater need for real spiritual

Hannahs in the kingdom than today. The coming battle of this day is one for the regeneration of our women and girls. I haven't much confidence in the outcome so long as some of our women dress and act as they do. Carlyle declared, "No great man ever had a fool for a mother." There is no sin in the most approved customs of society. But a slouch and filth are an abomination in the sight of the Lord. There must be a change; there must be reform along some lines. When five of our great college presidents, six editors of outstanding daily papers, and the greatest statesmen in America say in effect that "certain habits must be dropped," we should listen. Philosophers and preachers have warned us, but the brass band has struck up, and we soon forget the message. We do not need feminine men, and we certainly do not want masculine women. A young woman asked a friend the other day, "Why is it that men stare at me and criticise me when I walk down the streets?" The friend replied, "The way you paint, and dress, and flirt, you invite it all." She was right. One year (1935) over one hundred thousand dollars were spent for cosmetics; no wonder men died of painters' colic!

Again, there are too many homes without children. Most divorces come from homes without children. If it were possible, there is not an angel of the skies but would feel honored with motherhood. Since God could not be on earth at all times, he gave unto us saintly women and mothers instead. There are some hotels today that will not let a woman with a babe in her arms stay all night but they will let a woman with a sore-eyed dog stay, and they will furnish her a valet for the dog. The roughest human God ever made knows enough to stand back when he launches a new-born soul into the world.

Look at our women burn up cigarettes, take God's name in vain, and blush not at a cocktail. I could not say that a lady would not do these things, because someone might quickly take issue with me; but I will say that God Almighty's type of a lady will not. When a mother lets her little girl at the impressionable age of fourteen, fifteen, or sixteen years go out to a picture show, dance, or auto ride and come in at twelve or one o'clock, is she not contributing to the moral delinquency of her own daughter?

There is nothing finer or grander than for a boy or girl to have a sweetheart upon reaching the age of maturity; and the best place to find a sweetheart is in the church. But, mother, guide and protect that child, for she is almost helpless, so young.

Another shameful sight is to see one of these, "has beens," "seen better days," "fading roses," "old cackling hens" all dolled up and dressed like a peacock trying to come back, while all the world sings, "She ain't what she used to be."

So long as parents obey their children, turn their training over to the nurse or some other proxy, juvenile courts will go on. As one remarked, "Save the parents and you save the children." If a mother has lost all control over her boy, what preacher can influence him? The home needs Jesus. And many a boy needs a home and a mother more than anything else.

Think of it! Over two thousand boys and girls were in juvenile courts one year (1935). These young people were not from homes whose only Bible was a deck of cards and whose only prophet was a flask of whiskey but from homes like gilded palaces. It's the crimes of the rich which shock us. We need women today who, like Mary, will find time to sit at the feet of Jesus and learn of him. We need mothers who, like Hannah of old, will pray and say of their children, "As long as he liveth, he is thine."

A man never goes to hell so fast as when things go wrong in the home; and a man never goes to heaven so fast as when things go right in the home.

It would be better to send a *Titanic* out upon the deep without a rudder or a pilot than to launch a home without Jesus Christ and a hallowed, Christian influence. What influence is comparable to the influence of a godly woman in the home? President McKinley said of his mother, "My angel"; Carlyle said of his wife, "The peace of God came into my soul when I looked into your eyes." One of America's most illustrious statesmen, when on a visit to the grave of his mother, and as tears flowed down his cheeks, prayed, "Oh, mantle of Mother, fall on me; Mother's God be my God." When Joseph was tempted by Potiphar's wife, doubtless he thought of the vision he had received at his trundle bed, at his mother's knee—the vision of a clean life—and said, "I cannot do this evil in thy sight."

You have heard of Frances Willard, Susan Wesley, and Queen Victoria, but you have never heard of the uncrowned queen of my life—my mother. She was unknown outside the circle where she lived. She did not have many city airs and ways. She was just an old-fashioned Christian lady. If I could gather all the adjectives from all the languages of the world together and arrange them into a rhetorical bouquet; if I could walk through all the flower gardens of all time and gather flowers of thornless beauty and tie them into a wreath of imperishable fragrance; select, as one has said, the richest jewels that ever flashed in a monarch's crown and build a monument high as the skies, covering its head with a halo of glory and liquid sunshine, Mother of mine, they should all be thine.

Earth hath some beautiful spots, but none so lovely as where mother sleeps.

When we think of her sacrifices, her untiring devotion, her prayers, and her faith, and then think of her waiting up yonder for us, in the land where the leaves never fade and the sun never sinks, we cannot help but sing, "Tell mother I'll be there."

ARE YOU FOR UNCLE SAM?

If I forget thee, O Jerusalem.—PSALM 137:5.

Jerusalem was the home of David, and America is our home. America is one of time's greatest miracles. Just a few years ago we were like a babe wrapped in swaddling clothes, trying to run a great race. Look at the miracle. We had to fight for years to secure European recognition. We had an army in the Revolutionary War that numbered less than twenty-five thousand soldiers. We won the praise of the Old World not by our army and navy but by the character of our citizenship, the manhood and womanhood of our country. Our credit was impaired. We had a paper currency that was almost worthless. Carpetbaggers and grafters were everywhere. One-fifth of our population were members of the Negro race. Tom Paine's *The Age of Reason* had a large circulation, and for a time it looked as if this land which the Pilgrims had dedicated to God would become atheistic, but Roger Williams, John Wesley, and others were yet to be heard from, and God's truth, like Pershing's army, was marching on.

Who can study the God-illuminating history of America and not see the hand of God guiding the ark of the American covenant? We are ever proud of our forefathers, and we know that, with all our embellishments in our brightest hours, we are not the men and women they were. What a nation! What an empire for one flag to wave over! As Bryan said, "A nation where every man is a king and every woman a queen, but no one desires to wear the crown."

But America seems not to be so beautiful today. The black flag of crime and sin waves triumphantly over this land of churches. The sabbath is commercialized, and thousands pay no more attention to it than a last year's almanac. All our sacred and holy days have been turned into bacchanalian feasts. We license almost every evil for the sake of the almighty dollar. Children can't walk the streets without being exposed to ten thousand temptations. We pray to God to end depressions, stop forest fires, stay drouths and dust storms, and then turn around and vote to unloose hell.

Even marriage is a vulgar show many times, and burials are often dress parades. Divorce is rampant. Such conditions are not only killing men and women but also slaughtering children.

Communism and socialism are our greatest swaggering braggarts. God has taken America in for a licking. We are digging our own graves, lighting our own fuses, and manufacturing our own dynamite.

If You Are for Uncle Sam, You Must Stand for the Supremacy of the People—all the people. That is true Americanism—the right of the majority to rule. The safety of the highest is bound up in the safety of the lowest. Our motto must be, "All for one, and one for all." We cannot forget our great national trinity: the Magna Charta, the Declaration of Independence, and the Constitution of the United States.

Armies and navies today cannot hold men back, nor can humanity be fed from a common crib. As Woodrow Wilson said, "The people are in the saddle now." New York with its Tammany gang and Philadelphia with its Matt Quay hoodlums cannot vote people in a mass today as you would herd sheep. Ours is a government of the people. It is not the preacher, nor the priest, nor the church, nor the dictator, but the people. What is sovereign power? Sovereign power is not Congress, nor the President, nor the Supreme Court; it's t-h-e p-e-o-p-l-e. To the people is the last appeal, and their word is final.

Caste, intolerance, class distinction, and race hatred must go. We cannot pat ourselves on the back and think we are free from prejudice. No section of the land can claim a monopoly on racial bitterness. In the South it may be the white man and the Negro; and in the West the native son and the Japanese; in the East the capitalist and laboring man; and in the North all combined. New York, Chicago, and Boston do not practice social equality with the Negro any more than Atlanta, Memphis, or Birmingham. Look at South Side Chicago—thirty years ago one great white spot. Soon a few thousand Negroes from Alabama, Georgia, and the Carolinas came north and settled on the South Side—and what a black spot it is today! The whites moved out, and even turned their mansions and churches over to the Negroes and moved miles away. Taxpayers and property owners once protested vigorously against selling to a Negro a home in the Capitol Hill district in Denver drawing the same color line as they do in Dixie.

The seat for the greatest riots today is not in Atlanta, Nashville, or Birmingham, but in New York City, Chicago, and Detroit. The damnatory creed should go. America cannot stand for the blackguard, ward politician, mudslinger, or race castigator. I tell you, swaggering braggadocio, jingoism, and quarrelsome blusterism, are not Americanism nor patriotism.

This is a day of love, co-operation, federation, alliance, nationalism, and togetherness. War is the wildest insanity that ever burned in the bosom of any soul. The dying words of General Grant, chiseled in stone on his great monument on Riverside Drive in New York City, must be America's message to all combatants—"Let us have peace."

Thank God for a Christ who laid one hand upon the shoulder of the broadclothed millionaire and the other hand upon the shoulder of the man in humble raiment; then slowly, sweetly, and gently, by his death on the cross, brought them together through faith in his saving grace and united them with heaven's marriage ceremony, "As ye would that men should do to you, do ye also to them." That's Americanism, respecting and considering the rights of all; even standing in the other fellow's place.

If You Are for Uncle Sam, You Must Stand for the Supremacy of Law and Order. What a sad commentary upon our manhood to have someone say, "The law cannot be enforced." Governor Folk of Missouri proved that the law could be enforced even after the police, militia, and the constabulary had failed to do it. But the laws will not be enforced so long as we let the gamblers, brewers, and lawless elect men to office. I'll never forgive New York State for saying, through its legislature, after an overwhelming number of states had adopted the Eighteenth Amendment, "We will not enforce the Eighteenth Amendment." They seceded from the Constitution; yet no state hurled greater criticism and sarcasm against South Carolina when it withdrew or refused to obey the Constitution than did New York. If he who fired a shot at Fort Sumter was an enemy to the Constitution of the United States of America, how about the man who says, "I will not obey the Eighteenth or Seventeenth or Sixteenth Amendment"? Assuming such an attitude is no less than treason. If one has a right to pick out what part of the Constitution he will obey, then what becomes of the Constitution? It will be nothing more than a football.

Take prohibition—it did not fail; the Federal Government failed to enforce it. If one-third the effort had been made to enforce it as was made to destroy it, it would have been a godsend to the nation. What can we think of an officer of the law, wearing a badge, brass buttons, and going around criticising the law that he swore before God to enforce?

And we certainly are not enforcing the law under repeal. Sanford Bates, the head of our Federal prisons, had to admit there was no improvement. When the leading liquor and brewery advocate in America says, "Unless we look out, prohibition will be back in ten years," I know it must be damnable.

Is America headed hellward? Are we in a mad race for "freelovism"? Think of the once leading lady of the land suggesting that if girls want to drink and smoke, it might be all right to do so if done in moderation. No wonder the W. C. T. U. protested. Here is the main reason law is not enforced.

In one of our leading cities, four cases were being tried in Federal court. A poor Greek, convicted of selling bootleg, was sentenced to one hundred days in jail and two hundred dollars fine. A poor Negro convicted for the same offense was sentenced to one hundred days and two hundred dollars fine. In the same court, at the same time, and with the same judge, the Elks Club and a leading hotel charged with the same offense,bootlegging, had their cases dismissed by paying a fifty dollar fine each. What a travesty upon law and order?

If You Are for Uncle Sam, You Must Stand for the Supremacy of His Ideals and Institutions. The broadest platform upon which any man can stand is found in the simple declaration, "I am an American." Any man, regardless of race, creed, or condition, who stands for the flag, should receive our right hand of fellowship; and any man, be he Catholic, Jew, or Protestant, who does not put God Almighty first, and Uncle Sam next—well, this country should be too small for him. He should pull for Uncle Sam or pull out. I have more respect for the 100 per cent Bolshevik than for a fifty-fifty, hyphenated, half-baked American.

We have in this country as many "isms" as Heinz's famous varieties. We have communism, fascism, Hitlerism, and bolshevism; but there is room in this country for only one "ism" and that is Americanism. In our flag there is centered the interest of home, church, and government; and if that flag goes down, this nation becomes a hell on earth.

We made an irrevocable mistake when, in an unguarded moment, we said to the downtrodden of all the earth, "Come and rest beneath the shade of our tree of liberty." God be thanked for that large number who came here to escape the despotism of Prussianized thrones. There are no better Americans in America. But with these millions came a disreputable throng who had no higher object than to trample our institutions in the mud and mire. I do not believe our forefathers meant for this land of milk and honey to be the dumping ground for the filth of the old world; the shrine at which the godless of all realms should worship. Our fathers never meant for us to spread a table of good things, have them eat the fat of the land, and then turn around and bite the hand that fed them. In response to our invitation they came to these shores not only to live, make their bread and butter, but demanding the franchise—the right to vote. I know Henry Ward Beecher said, "Let them come, we will assimilate them." But have we? They are crowding us to the wall. The foreign birthrate is an alarming fact. Read the *Vanishing American*—How the birthrate is almost two to one among foreign married couples as compared to American married couples. How long will this be the land of the free and the home of the brave? What mean these great temples being built to Buddha and Mahomet in this country? Hear me—unless we Americanize, Christianize, and evangelize these people, they will paganize us. It's no time to be pussy-footed, frozen stiff, mealy-mouthed, and spineless. So long as there are more Jews in New York City than are in Palestine, and more Irish than are in Ireland, it will not be a question of, What does the American want in New York City? but, What does the foreigner want? Go to some of our great cities on the Fourth of July or on other national holidays and see the foreign flags floating in the breeze. Not so in Rome, Paris, London, or Russia.

I believe I have a panacea for our political and economic troubles. I want the time to come, when no man, be he black or white, rich or poor, great or small, will ever be given the franchise until he can read and write the Constitution of the United States and swear allegiance to the American flag. Stand by your country. It's my America, right or wrong.

If You Are for Uncle Sam, You Must Stand for the Christian's God, the Christian Religion, and the Christian Church. The founding of this nation was an appeal to Almighty God, and so must its salvation be. "When the righteous are in authority, the people rejoice: but when the wicked beareth rule, the people mourn." We have had the mourning. From all quarters of the nation comes the cry, "Where now is the God of Elijah?"

Will Rogers was right when he said, "You may blame Hoover, Roosevelt, the Republicans, or the Democrats; we had it coming to us." Mr. Babson declared (referring to the depression of the early 30's), "The depression

will not end until there is a great spiritual awakening."
Nothing can make America safe for democracy, and
democracy safe for America, except the centripetal and
centrifugal force of religion. Remove your churches,
and real estate would not be worth as much as real estate
in Hades. The church gives protection to all we have,
and it is the cheapest protection we pay for. Sometimes
we make fun of the church; call her creeds "blue laws,"
her followers "longwhiskered fanatics." We hear the
cry, "Do not make our city a 'Sunday school'"; but note
this: Los Angeles, Detroit, and Long Beach, the three
fastest growing cities in America in 1935, are also the
three strongest church-going cities in the nation. Show
me what a brothel, saloon, or gambling hell ever did for
a person? I'll tell you what they have done for every
one of their slaves: given them a red nose, a foul breath,
an empty stomach, a pair of patched breeches, and a
ticket straight to hell.

Who wants to live in godless, Christless, and almost
churchless Russia, Spain, or Mexico? It is strange that
Bob Ingersoll, the hired defamer of the Christian's God,
lived in Illinois, the strongest state in the Union for
churches. If it had not been for the restraining hand of
the church, the Bolsheviks would have had this country
long ago and we would be making brick without straw
or water.

A great general uttered a real truth when he said,
"I shall have no fear for America so long as I can hear
one hundred thousand church bells ring out God's praises
every Sunday morning." Another great general, General
Foch, in assuming command of all the Allied armies in
World War I, turned to his soldiers and said, "What
France needs is Jesus Christ!"

O America, the beautiful; child whose cradle God's
hand did rock; youth whose hands are full of freedom's

fruit—you need Christ! The coming revival will not only be one of American patriotism, manhood, and womanhood but a revival that will and must enthrone Christ as King of kings and Lord of all.

ARE YOU RIDING THE BLIND BAGGAGE?

He that is not with me is against me.—Matthew 12:30.

Many are asking the questions, Can I be a Christian outside the church?—Can I go to heaven and not be a church member?—Does the church save? I can answer by asking what kind of a Democrat or Republican would a man be outside his party? What kind of a Mason outside the lodge? What kind of an American would a foreigner make unless naturalized? If I have the money, I can buy a ticket to Chicago, ride the streamline train, eat my meals in the diner, and in all probability I'll get there. The other way is to ride the blind baggage or ride the brakes. I may get there, but it's a mighty dirty, dangerous, dusty, and cheap way to travel.

Yes, you may get to heaven outside the church, but isn't it a selfish and uncertain way to travel? While a mother does not save you, all acknowledge that a mother is a priceless blessing. The church does not save you, but the church is a spiritual mother. You should believe in an equal distribution of the burdens of society and want to claim your share. I refuse to be a blind baggage rider. What kind of a man is he who accepts the blessings the church provides and the protection it gives his home, government, or person, and does not want to do his share? I do not mean financially—bootleggers would give all the money we need to run the churches. I mean the giving of one's influence and example.

We can prove that the church contributes a protection of commercial, civic, and moral values, sought in vain elsewhere. But for Christianity we might not be wearing clothing; but, like Nebuchadnezzar, eating grass as does the ox, or eating one another. What caused tiny Japan to arouse its latent powers and walk up and box the jaws of enormous China? The ruler of Japan leaned heavily upon the shoulders of a godly missionary, and through his advice and instruction sent different deputations to this country to examine our buildings, battleships, etc. They returned and duplicated what they saw, and Japan today is what it never would have been without Christianity. Dr. R. J. Willingham said when he visited Honolulu forty years ago, that his life was worth nothing on the streets without a bodyguard. Fifteen years ago he returned to Honolulu, and said, "My life was just as safe as in any American city." What made the difference? On every hillside was a little red schoolhouse and a church.

What infidel today wants to live in a godless, Christless, churchless city or nation? Strangely, Bob Ingersoll hated the church, yet he lived in Illinois, the greatest state in the Union for churches. The story is told that one night after Bob had finished his tirade against the church, he shouted, "Name one thing the church has ever done for this state." "If you can answer that, hold up your hand." An old lady held up her hand, and he said, "All right, sister, tell us what the church ever did for this state." And the old woman cried out, "Kept you from becoming governor—goody."

What infidel living today would be willing to go back and live in the so-called brilliant years of history when Cato publicly commended young men for entering houses of pollution. What we consider vice he considered virtue; and what we call virtue he called vice. When Paris discarded the religion of Christ, the reign of terror started. I'm convinced that Lot's palatial mansion in Sodom was not worth half as much as Abraham's tent in the wilderness. Would it not have been better for Lot had he brought his children up under the religious tutelage of Abraham than to pay the price he did? Even his children mocked him in the end.

Let me give you three pictures of a world without a church. In a thinly settled portion of Pennsylvania years ago, a man hung up a sign with these words on it, "This Farm For Sale." A stranger passing asked the price. The farmer replied, "I have tried to get ten thousand for it, but the first fellow who gives me five thousand, the place is his." The stranger gasped, "Five thousand; you couldn't build that house for ten thousand, let alone all the land." "I know it, stranger," the farmer answered, "but I have advertised it for a long time and I can't get a bite. I'm twenty miles from a church and a schoolhouse."

Your property wouldn't be worth as much as property in Sodom except for the church.

One tells us that land in Turkey is the richest on earth; yet we had rather own the poorest acre of land in America than the richest in Turkey. What gives our land its value?—the schools and churches.

A church was about to be sold under the sheriff's hammer, and an infidel paid the mortgage. When asked why, he replied, "That little church is worth more to the morale of my people than the entire police force of this city." Isn't the church God's spiritual standing army, his miniature police force? In Los Angeles at Seventh and Broadway, I saw the greatest congestion of cars I had ever seen. The police on that corner had to leave to quell a disturbance, and immediately there were thousands of cars in a jam for blocks distant. Whistles, horns, and sirens blew, and human throats yelled and screamed. Each tried to get an inch or a foot ahead of the other fellow. They tried to push, crowd, and turn one another to the side. I said then, "What a picture of a city without a church." What the prophet said is still true: "Men would devour each other" if there were no churches.

We have been told that it costs more to support courthouses, police, and jails than it does to run the church. I think all are with me so far, but somehow I seem to hear the shrill cry, Why organization? Men want to be free lancers; they refuse to accept any kind of authority. They want to be their own drum major—their own brass band. Let me answer the question, Why organization? Labor unions, trades, professions, and sporting leagues are all organized—even the saloons, gamblers, and all the underworld are organized to a man. There is also a national tramp association—all tramps are organized, except some religious tramps.

Jesus did not say, "Where one saint is gathered together," but "where two or three." Hermits live by themselves; but who wants to be a hermit or a savage?

In World War I the American soldiers were in France one year before they were allowed to fire a shot? They went over there to fight; their hands ached to pull the trigger. General Pershing took those one million raw recruits and for one solid year trained, developed, organized, and disciplined them, and one morning announced that the first American Expeditionary Army was ready. General Pershing shouted, "Forward, march!" and one million men stepped forth as one man, and every Prussianized throne trembled, and that day despotism went to hell shouting, "The Watch on the Rhine."

There must be organization, for what you cannot do alone you can do by working in concert with others. It was said of one great American that he would not take part in anything unless he could be "the bridegroom at every wedding and the corpse at every funeral." I have heard that in Massachusetts the "Lodges spoke only to Cabots, and the Cabots spoke only to God." Think of a Christian serving God all by himself. What he condemns is wrong and what he condones is right. What super-selfishness and egotism that is! Let me tell you that the organized church is the only thing that hell will listen to. These "isms" and cults are too fanatical, puritanical, and lopsided to have any kind of a hearing. Just show me one reform, one single national blessing one of these off-side brands of religion ever gave to the world.

First. Many say, "I am a blind baggage rider because there are too many churches." Yes, but the churches are nearer together than any other institution. Strange to say, the man who always brings that charge usually is a member of several secret orders. Yes, we have one hundred and twenty various faiths in this country, but we also have over one thousand secret organizations. Different denominations are as necessary to American life as different political parties. That charge is only a scapegoat to dodge responsibility.

Second. Men are saying the church is full of grafters, and so they stay out. Look at Billy Sunday and Jack Dempsey as illustrations. In Toledo Jack Dempsey made about two hundred thousand dollars in twenty minutes. At the same time Billy Sunday was holding a meeting in New York City—not for just twenty minutes, but eight long weeks, finally wearing himself out so completely that he was forced to go to Mayo's. The meeting paid him one hundred thousand dollars, and he gave every cent of it to the Red Cross. Isn't a preacher of righteousness worth more to the world than a Joe Louis, a Max Baer, a Jack Dempsey or a Max Schmeling?

THIRD. Here comes another who says, "I am a blind baggage rider because there are too many hypocrites in the church." A woman said to me one day, "I'm not in the church, I pick my crowd." Didn't she pick a fine crowd—millions of bootleggers, prostitutes, gamblers, and gangsters? What a crowd to gang with! Yes, there are hypocrites in the church, but I'll find you ten outside the church to one you will find inside. When a man yells "Hypocrites in the church," I wonder, after all, if he is not seeing in the hypocrite a true reflection of himself. Why does any man want to measure himself with a skin-flint, weasly runt, nickel-plated, hard-boiled, run-down-at-the-heel church member? Why not compare yourself to the saints in Israel? Perhaps you would look as Billy Sunday once said, "Like a rat terrier beside an elephant." Methinks that if we would sweep in front of our own door, our neighbor's door would look better.

I want to answer two questions that are persistently asked by blind baggage riders.

First, what has the church ever done to help mankind? I can prove that all you are and have the church gave you. Let's make an inventory.

How about America? The Pilgrims dedicated this country to God and to the church. If the church could offer nothing else, is not America a worthy trophy? It was the church that paved the way for higher education for women. Who gave this country woman suffrage? How about the public schools? What institution ever produced such a gift? Who gave you religious liberty? The very fact that you can live in this country and be an infidel and not go to any church you owe that right to the church. During the days of the Thirteen Colonies you could be jailed if you stayed away from church three consecutive Sundays. Sometimes I wish we had such a law now. Where did Masonry come from? Every degree and every password came from the Bible. Ministers and scores of Christians gave up their lives to save and defend the Bible. Had the church not preserved the Bible, there would be no Masonic lodge today. Masons, how can you desert your old mother, the church? Odd Fellows, Knights of Pythias, Rebeccas, Eastern Stars—you all owe a debt of gratitude to the Bible for your existence.

Marriage was never placed on its high pedestal and the practice of polygamy stopped until the church asserted her influence. In many places motherhood was considered a disgrace, and the world never appreciated childhood until Jesus declared, "Of such is the kingdom of heaven." On Sunday over one hundred thousand church bells ring, and millions attend Sunday schools. I challenge any lodge or institution to produce the equal of our Bible schools. What is the best and truest friend mankind has today?—the sabbath. Russia believes in no sabbath, no church, no God. The church gives you all. A man said to me, "You are mistaken, I did not get my principles from the church." I asked, "Where did you get them?" He replied, "I got them from my mother." I said, "Right you are, but where did your mother get them? From the church—for she was one of my best members."

All roads lead back to the church. I know the church has sinned, been wounded, even been disgraced by her supposed friends; yet, with all the mistakes, she is still the grandest institution on earth. When we think of the imperfect people who have come into its folds and the imperfect hands that have built her walls, what a great temple we have! The difference between the church and every other institution is that the church picks folks up where others throw them down. The invitation of others is, "Come ye highest, come ye best, come ye purest"; but the church adds this invitation, "Come ye

sinners, come ye lost, come ye unworthy." If the dirtiest bootlegger, gambler, or reprobate on earth were to walk down the aisle of a church and say, "I am saved, Christ is my Saviour," there is not a church that could shut her doors against him.

How can you accept all these gifts I have mentioned and force your mother, wife, friends, and all the rest of us to keep the church going and you not bear your burden? Was there ever a more consummate piece of selfishness?

Let me answer the second question: Was Christ a member of the church, and was the New Testament church organized?

Christ was a member of the only organization in existence at that time for the dissemination of truth. At twelve years of age he was found in the Temple confounding the doctors. We read, "As his custom was, he went into the synagogue." Can you be a Christian outside the church? Christ calls the church "his bride." Can you be a Christian and ignore the "bride of Christ"? The Word says that he died for the church and shed his blood for it. Can you belong to him and ignore his death and shed blood? Paul says, "Husbands, love your wives, even as Christ also loved the church." Christ calls the church "his body." Christ said, "If thy brother shall trespass against thee, . . . if he will not hear thee, . . . tell it unto the church."

Yes, they were organized. The early church had bishops, evangelists, stewards, elders, deacons, pastors, and they were all elected by the church. Acts 15 says the church had a great convention in Jerusalem, and its various units sent messengers and delegates. Most certainly there was organization. The New Testament even names some of the pastors of the churches. Christ had some degree of organization, for we read of the twelve, the 70, the 500; and he even had his inner and

outer circle. In Acts 14:23: "They had ordained them elders in every church." In 1 Corinthians 12:28: "And God hath set some in the church, first, apostles, secondarily prophets thirdly teachers." There's organization for you. The church is called the assembly of the saints, not saint.

Blind baggage rider, you haven't one leg to stand on. I am proud to be a member of the church because it's the only institution that keeps the sense of God organized in the community; because it affords me the finest opportunity of earth for Christian service; because I can do much more by acting in concert with others than alone; because Christ loved the church and submitted to its ordinances; because I am giving my example and influence for the growth and maintenance of the grandest of all temples, the temple of Christianity.

"He that is not with me is against me." I wonder, after all, if what another has said is not true—"if the church would be more imperfect when its critics came in." If all had acted as some of those today who are fighting a guerrilla warfare, conducting a bushwhacking campaign, a spiritual insurrection, seeming to be religious anarchists, crime would have folded its wings long ago over the grave of a God who had been dethroned. If we are to live together in heaven, why not try it down here? The church was good enough for our mothers, fathers, the saints, the prophets, and apostles. Why shouldn't it satisfy us? All these cults, "isms" and "side-track" religions would never have been heard from save for the church.

Don't be a blind baggage rider, a spiritual caterpillar; but let your fires burn on our altars, bind your heart together with ours and join in singing with all the redeemed of God:

"I love Thy Church, O God!
  Her walls before Thee stand,
Dear as the apple of Thine eye,
  And graven on Thy hand.

For her my tears shall fall;
  For her my prayers ascend;
To her my cares and toils be given,
  Till toils and cares shall end."

WHAT'S THE MATTER WITH THE AMERICAN HOME?

As for me and my house, we will serve the Lord.—
JOSHUA 24:15.

Many want a great sphere in which to serve God.
Why not try the home? What a call for consideration
and fair play! Two wills, dispositions, and tempera-
ments. Life's greatest trinity is fatherhood, motherhood,
and childhood. We need a new pedagogy taught in our
colleges; to have a chair endowed that will teach the
scientizing of human hearts and lives. I am not surprised
that long after the drums of the Civil War had ceased
to beat, and the cannons were spiked, and the smoke of
battle cleared away, the soldiers of Grant on one side
of the Appomattox and the soldiers of Lee on the other,
all sang together, "Be it ever so humble, there's no place
like home."

Tomorrow, millions of men and women will go forth
to toil, work, and sacrifice for the sake of loved ones at
home. I want to speak of a few minor sins that are
breaking up the American home, and then of a few
major sins that are wrecking it.

FIRST. Many are compromising with sin, winking
at evil, minimizing sin, and excusing wrongdoing. Sin
is not mortal error, an innocent hallucination, a night-
mare, a man of straw, a passing fancy, or merely a creature of the preacher's imagination. Sin is the most terrific
fact in God's universe. It is written in letters of tears and
blood. It is as real as brick, mortar, and stone.

Persuade men to believe there is no sin, no hereafter, no heaven or hell, no rewards or punishments in the next world, and lust will become natural, murder and insanity dodge, the wife become a mistress or a servant, the home a place to hang out, and the dirtiest rake that walks the streets of the city will be on the same footing for eternity with your mother, the dearest of all women.

Strange, but men who will excuse one sin will go right on through the category of evil excusing all sin. They defend all kinds of iniquity—gambling, red light districts, illegal sale of whiskey, and some defend suicide. Others even defend Judas Iscariot and tell us what a hero he was in the part he played in the great drama of Christianity.

Sin is no enraptured dream of a poet's fancy, no whim, no peaceful sleep of a charmed Orpheus. There is absolutely no romance or glamor to it.

Nothing enslaves, scorches, sears, stings, and damns like sin. You can't use moral suasion on sin any more than you can use moral suasion on lions and tigers.

SECOND. I think that the neglect of the Bible has played its part in the wreckage of the home. William Jennings Bryan once said in my pulpit, "Trot out a book that has a better record back of it than the Bible and I'll accept it." No wonder Victoria shouted, "That Book is the explanation why the sun never sets on my empire!" What has the Koran ever done for Turkey?— the Talmud for Palestine?—the Veda for the Hindus?— or ancestral worship for China?—all pigmy nations.

Hear me! I defy any home to read the Bible daily, keep the sabbath, have family prayer, and pay God his tenth and not make a success of it. The first Psalm, the Ten Commandments, and the twenty-fifth chapter of Matthew still play an important part on the consciences of men. One great soul declared, "The only objection to the Bible is a bad life."

THIRD. The wild scramble for money contributes its part in breaking up homes today. Money has its place. God bless the man who owns money, but heaven pity the man money owns. Money in the hand is fine, but money in the heart is serious. Nothing so reveals the inside of a man as does the almighty dollar. Thousands place their souls on the auction block and hold out their moneyized hands crying, "What will ye give me if I release Him unto thee?" Upon thousands of homes and hearts you could write, "Blasted by the god of gold," "Sold into sin and shame." We could change the Scripture to read, "What the law could not do in that it was weak, it did through the power of money." Back of almost every war, murder, divorce, and moral issue is the almighty dollar. Many of us are round-shouldered because we have allowed the things of this world to weight us down, when God intended for us to walk with the world beneath our feet. To place money in the hand of a boy or girl who has not been trained in the wise spending of that money is like placing dynamite there. More have been damned by their riches than by their poverty.

FOURTH. Filthy literature and the yellow jingoism of sensational newspapers have helped to wreck many homes. I take off my hat to a great newspaper in Denver that has at the beginning of every article on crime in a special type this sentence, "Crime never pays." Another great daily I know of has segregated all crime articles and placed them on the fifth page rather than on the first and boils it down to less than one and a half columns. I can put the newspapers on the track of almost any good man or woman and in less than six months' time they can find or manufacture something suspicious about him or her.

FIFTH. The double standard of morals does its part. A woman has just as much right to hit the bright lights, drink, smoke, and swear as any man. The divorce mill will grind on, and alimony hunters, affinities, soul mates, blackmailers, and grass widows line our streets so long as we have laws and customs that are right for men and wrong for women.

Marriage is a partnership. The wife puts into that partnership as much as the husband. What man would change places with his wife? At times she gives her very life. Should the woman in a home be the servant or understudy of the man? Should she be the one the husband supports? There should certainly be an understanding between the two regarding the pocketbook. We swore at the marriage altar, "With this ring I thee do wed and all my worldy goods bestow." Do not make the home a place of servitude for the wife.

SIXTH. Sabbath desecration overthrows the home, church, school, and all. Destroy the sabbath and free speech, free schools, free religion, and our star will forever set. God most certainly has a right to one day in seven. It seems that every sacred day we have—Christmas, Thanksgiving, Memorial Day, Easter have all been taken by the hands of sinful men and crucified upon the tree of sinful pleasure and indulgence. Any nation which robs God of his sabbath will pay a fearful price. Russia or any other nation will not escape. Do away with our American sabbath, its church bells, Bible schools, holy hours of worship, and never again will we be able to sing, "America, the Beautiful."

SEVENTH. I believe the motion picture industry has done more to wreck the home than any other agency.

After you say all you can in favor of the movies—and some things can be said for them—they still remain the most God-dishonoring, sabbath-breaking, divorce-breeding, crime-feeding, home-wrecking institution in America.

An actress or an actor can sink to the lowest hell and it does not seem to hurt her or him. The blacker and more foul their names, the more the theaters will be packed to see them. We would not stand for it in our schools, our teachers, our preachers, nor even our servants.

We legislate against undesirables, quarantine contagious diseases, exclude filthy literature (at least, some of it), yet permit the profanity, vulgarity, lewdness, and indecency of the screen with all its slime and pitch to fall upon us and our children. We permit many pictures to be shown that many foreign countries would not allow within their borders. The front pages of your newspapers have in recent years reported outrageous episodes of some outstanding screen idols. Do you mean to tell me that the ministry should be silent when five great college presidents appointed to go to the bottom of this brought in a report of "guilty"; when the Catholic and the Federated Churches in America report "guilty"; when our great secret orders refuse to admit them. Isn't it time our Christian people said, "Away with them"?

You can't sit in a show thirty minutes without seeing cigarette smoking by the youngest, cocktail drinking, drunkenness, taking God's name in vain, some husband or wife discarded for another, the glorification of wrong, and finally a lot of sentimental gush. In the world of baseball Judge Landis banished the crooks and gamblers, and they have never returned. In political parties all cry, "Turn the rascals out!" and why not in the theatrical world drive these depraved actors and actresses out? I know why—the almighty dollar. So long as the industry is in the hands of these "golden calf" worshipers, you will never reform the motion picture business. You might just as well try to run a soda fountain in hell.

I know there have been and are the Will Rogerses, Wallace Beerys, Harold Lloyds, Joe Browns, Irvin Cobbs, George Arlisses, Grace Moores, Marie Dresslers and others who have been and are an honor to the profession; but look at the staggering percentage who have been divorced from one to five times and the scores who have been named guilty as corespondents. I am not pleading for the destruction of the stage and screen but for their regeneration and reformation. I do not want to see them become living brothels.

EIGHTH. How about gambling in the home? I do not play cards because it is against the rules of my church but because I have found in Christ something infinitely better. In every bootlegger's joint, gambling den, and other hellholes the one medium of vice is a deck of cards. Talk about them gambling with dominoes and checkers!—it's absurd and ridiculous—it's too tame. Just as well expect to see Strangler Lewis or Jimmy Braddock play postoffice.

Gambling in the homes is abhorrent today. In God's great Judgment Day, he will see no difference in the man who plays for a ten-dollar bill and the woman who plays for a piece of china or silver. It cannot be gambling for one and pleasure for the other. Heaven hasn't any favorites, half fares, or exemptions. Your boy would not go into a gambling hell; he would run from it, shun it as he would a viper. He would be absolutely afraid of it. But how about parlor gamblers? If you can keep your boy out of the hands of front-room gamblers and sometimes church gamblers, he will never enter a gambling den.

NINTH. Then there is the dance. If there is a more successful place for the white-slave dealer than the dance hall, it has never been discovered. We should vote out not only the saloons and gambling hells but two other incubuses of life, the dance hall and the vile pool halls.

At one time, when the mayor of Chicago, with the police, constabulary, and militia, could not stop the crime wave, he closed every pool hall and dance hall for one month, and Chicago had a new birth overnight. Ask your chief of police in any city where he first looks for a criminal.

I think the most disgusting and obscene thing you can witness is the position assumed by many in the modern dance. Who can defend it? If you will separate the sexes, I'll never say another word against dance, for I would not have to; it would go out of business as fast as any tornado. You say let the men dance with the men. In the language of another, "they would just as soon hug a lamppost, a barrel of pickles, or their mother-in-law."

I am a coward; anyone could whip me. But even a coward will fight at times. Just let me see any man assume the position with my wife that he does on the ballroom floor, cheek to cheek, breast to breast, and almost lip to lip, and when I am through with him he'll need a hospital or I'll need a hearse. All the hugging my wife gets I'll give her.

One of the leading physicians of America, before a great service club during Child Welfare Week, said, "It's the sex question that keeps most of our dances alive, and the position of the modern dance must go." (I'll send you his name if you wish.) I care more for his opinion than that of all the "flapper-snappers". You say, "Why not chaperon the dance"? If there is no harm in the dance, why chaperon it? You don't have to chaperon a parent-teachers' meeting, a lodge, or prayer meeting. When a dancing masters' convention says, "We must reform our business," it's time we quit defending it. The matron of the Florence Crittendon Home in Los Angeles said to me one day, "If any of your members believe there is no harm in the modern dance, just let them come out and talk to one hundred of my girls and I'll convince them."

So many say, "Our dances are respectable." It's the respectable sins that I'm afraid of. Many who are rich have the money to cover up—and how many sins money will cover and hush up! I am more concerned about the sins of those who live in brownstone fronts than the sins of those who live in the hovels below.

Lastly, the remedy and way out of all these temptations is Jesus. Our boys and girls have too many temptations to face as they walk the streets. Mother, father, is your influence and example best for the boy and girl? In the hereafter will your boy or girl say, "I cannot ever remember hearing my father or mother pray"?

When a small boy, I used to visit my grandfather's home. He was a Presbyterian elder, and before bedtime there was always family prayer—and how he prayed for me! I may not have appreciated it then—it seemed to bore me—but, let me say today, if I wanted to make a shipwreck of my faith and go to hell, I could not do it with the vision of my grandfather down on his knees before the throne of God praying for my salvation.

The roughest soul on earth or the most degenerate cannot get away from mother's God and Christ. What is comparable to a home anchored to Christ?

THE CITY BEAUTIFUL

And I John saw the holy city.—REVELATION 21:2.

Heaven is not an association, a memory, a condition, a past experience, or a mirage, but a place. The Bible calls it a "city" and speaks of its gates and streets, its choir, its thrones, its mansions. It is no phantasmagoria, and John says he saw it. I love to think of heaven as a home. A city always has homes and mansions, and the Bible says there are many there.

If you haven't a home of your own, surely you have not forgotten the home of your childhood. Today it may be nothing but a recollection, but every room is corniced with hallowed memories, and angels seem to upholster it before your eyes. It was the only place you could tell of your defeats and triumphs at the close of each day without being misunderstood. Stand with the soldier amid shot and shell and ask him where the jewels cluster the brightest, and he will answer, "Home, sweet home." Ask the President, as he kisses the Holy Bible and assumes his office, What is the Gibraltar of America? and hear him answer, "Home, sweet home."

That home may be in old Kentucky, whose carpet is the bluegrass and whose covering is God's liquid sunshine. It may be far down in Florida, amid a wealth of life and prodigality of growth, where the flowers seem to rival the beauty of the stars. It may be in stately Maine, or the prairies of Kansas, the oil fields of Oklahoma or Texas, the cotton fields of Carolina, the wheat fields of Minnesota, or in the roar of machinery in Ohio or Pennsylvania, or corn-covered Indiana. It may be in cool Colorado, the playground for the tired sons of toil, or among the tall eucalyptus trees in California. Somewhere is the home of the long ago, and our hearts beat a little faster as we think about it.

Ah, you living here in America may have your homes and mansions with their bay windows, conservatory windows, skylight windows, cathedral windows, and illuminated windows, but there is one window that will always be opened, and that one faces back to the home of long ago—Jerusalem, the fading.

I am not surprised to hear that many a Christian, before taking that last journey across the river never to return, takes his last look at the receding world and sweetly sings, "I'm going home to die no more." When I preach on heaven, I feel as if I were trying to paint an enduring picture out of mud, or, as a great preacher once said, "trying to illuminate a golden sunset with a tallow candle." Who could ever imagine a city like the great metropolis of the skies? Think of a city without brick, mortar, or stone—no rich or poor folk there, no slums, no graft, no taxation, no unemployment, and no politics. There has never been a bank failure in heaven, no rise and fall of money market, and no one eking out an existence. Murders, divorces, and all violations of law are unheard of in heaven. The storms, earthquakes, drouths, and crop failures that we have here will be unknown there. It is the wonder of the age, a lasting Eureka, the Utopia of the soul. How could it be? Yet, nineteen hundred years ago God flung open its gates while the saints passed through singing as they marched to Zion, the beautiful city of God.

Another wonder about this city is that it is for all of every race, creed, or color, who have been saved by Christ. Jerusalem was for the Jews, Constantinople for the Turk, Rome for the Romans, and Athens for the

Athenians, but God's Beautiful Up Yonder is for *all*
Christ redeemed. All Mr. Ford's or Mr. Rockefeller's
money cannot buy a corner in the City where the sun
never sets, the leaves never fade, and inhabitants ne'er
grow old or weary. If money could purchase a seat there,
then the Negro doggerel would come true: "If religion
was a thing that money could buy, the rich would have
it all, and the poor would have to die."

There will be no snobs, no upper class, no aristocrats,
no highbrows in heaven. There will be no brownstone
fronts above and tenements below. In many of our cities
there are beautiful estates with signs, "Private Grounds,"
"No Admission," "Keep Out." Over the gates celestial,
in the City of the Skies, will be only one sign. "Whosoever will may enter." Methinks the applause for the
widow who gave her mite or the woman who wiped his
feet with the hair of her head will be as thunderous as
the applause for Peter, or Paul, or Moody, or Spurgeon,
who won thousands.

Who can forget the story related by Irvin Cobb? In
a city of a million people lived a doctor with a large
practice. His office was in a twenty-story skyscraper.
The depression came and robbed him of all. He moved
his office to the barn at the rear of his home. So poor
was he that he painted his own sign, with the words on
it, "Dr. Thomas Riley, Office Upstairs," and nailed it on
the barn door. He became the good Samaritan of the
community, going here and there helping the helpless.
One day he was missing, and some friends, climbing the
shaky stairs and beating down the door found God's
angel, the old doctor, cold in death. Only a few nights
before he had been out in the sleet and snow on a mission
of mercy, had taken cold, and died alone. Kind friends
buried him. That afternoon, following the service, it
dawned upon them that "a great oak in the forest" had

fallen and something should be done to perpetuate his memory. They said, "We will sell his horse and buggy and his instruments and put up a marble slab." But lo, all these had been sold to purchase a burial plot. An old drunk, sober for the first time in many years, said, "Follow me." Up to the barn they all went and the old drunk tore off the barn door and all followed him to the cemetery. There they planted the door with the inscription on it at the head of the grave. The thunders shook it, the lightning scorched it, the winds whipped it, the storms swayed it, and time wrinkled it, but could not efface or eliminate the words pointing to the skies, "Dr. Thomas Riley, Office Up Stairs."

I doubt not that in the City Foursquare a good God has many offices and mansions in heaven for some Dr. Thomas Rileys who went down in defeat and despair.

The third wonder about the Land of the Unclouded Skies is that it has no changes. Years ago, Cripple Creek and Leadville, Colorado were cities of thirty and forty thousand; now, two or three thousand. Business blocks and residences boarded up and falling to ruin. As I looked at them I said, "Has beens." Heaven will never be a "has been." It's beyond the reach of corroding time and the ravages of wear. There are no good and bad times in Glory. There are no antiques and souvenirs.

My greatest wonder about heaven is that we make little preparation for it. When I was a boy, we prayed, preached, and sang about "The Sweet By and By." I believe I know why we hear so little about it now— there are too many "heavens." To one, heaven is business; to another, society; to another, politics, or art, or money, or pleasure. There are too many heavens, and they have shut out the divine vista. I sometimes wonder if God has hung up a "For Rent" sign in our house of many mansions.

Why Do We Call It the Beautiful City? It is not beautiful because of its walls of jasper, enchanting landscapes, unbroken streams, or liquid sunshine. It is not beautiful because of its golden streets and golden harps —a heaven like that would become monotonous to the very angels. It would make heaven too material and mechanical. Heaven is no place of spiritual indolence but one of service. They praise him forever in the Holy City. Just before Dr. Ray Petty, a pastor in Kansas City, died, he turned to his pal, the doctor, and said: "It's all right, Charlie, I'll soon walk up to the Lord Jesus, salute him, and say, 'Here I am, Lord Jesus, ready for my next job.'" Heaven is just another voyage, another journey, another job.

Heaven Will Be the Beautiful City, because age will play no part there. No gray hairs, no cramped limbs, no failing eyesight, no slow heartbeats will be heard of there. The old will grow younger, and there will be no deadline. Why, there will not even be a wrinkled brow in heaven; no pensions or retirements. There will be no crutches, no sunsets, no dying autumns, no marchings weary, no "last round-ups." You will never see crepe on a doorknob or a funeral in heaven. The grave is not all. If Christ knows the sparrow's call, numbers the hairs of our heads, paints the cheek of the peach and the rose, and if he takes account of the birds of the air, will he not care for his own in the gloaming or when the frost of the winter years come? God's Word is sure.

It's a Beautiful City because there will be no night of mystery there. In heaven there will be no burning of midnight oil trying to solve unsolved problems. Oh, these mysteries! Why couldn't every day be a summer day? Why do mountains, seas, and gulfs separate people? Why couldn't the seas be plowed ground? Why couldn't this earth have been stationary instead of flying through space at the rate of a thousand miles a second? Why does righteousness wear rags and iniquity wear purple? Why is the tyrant on the throne and the good man in chains? Why is it when one man sins it follows him to the grave, and when another man sins, he goes through life unwhipped and blessings unsought fall upon his lap? Why does God permit sin? Why doesn't God kill the devil and put hell out of business? Why doesn't God make Denver the Holy City? Who can answer? How appalling the silence! But in heaven we will no longer see through a glass darkly, but face to face. Every day there will be a revelation day. We will know all about the hand that moved in darkness and gathered up isolated causes. We will be compelled to say, "Thou art just and right in all thy ways." It's not for poor man to ask God for any explanation, but to wait and murmur not until that day comes when God's saints go marching home.

It's the Beautiful City of God because the oldest inhabitant of the glory world will never see a tear. It must be that in some way God's hand wipes away all tears from the eyes so that the soul can see as if looking through a prism its future abode undimmed at the right or left hand of God's throne. No sob ever mingled in Eden's breeze. There will be no tears of disappointment, of ingratitude, of treachery, or of betrayal.

It's the Beautiful City of God because there is no suffering, no pain, no sorrow there. The problem of suffering is one that baffles the universe. Do sorrows run riot through the soul? Is it a fact that God does not care? Is he helpless in the presence of his decrees? One of the hardest questions I have ever tried to answer is the inquiry, "If your God is kind, good, benevolent, and beneficent, why does he permit sickness, sorrow, and death?" Why do we have Gethsemanes and Golgothas?

Dr. Talmadge gives a fine answer. He said: "God permits affliction, trials, and defeats to come into our lives to make us homesick for Glory. If we have our way, we would take a million years' lease on this life." How true! A man would rather live in poverty than die in luxury. Man will lay hold of anything that will prolong life? Let the storms come, for sometimes it takes the storm to reveal the Saviour's face. It takes the storm to lift us up out of our selfish life; and only the storm at times will break the bolts that lock Jesus Christ out of the heart.

A little girl going home late in the afternoon while the shadows gathered met a kind man who asked, "Little girl, aren't you afraid to go across the dark bridges and swamps?" She replied, "Yes, sir, but it's the way home." Could there be a better or more inspired answer? Let suffering, trials, defeats, and death come—it's the way home. Behind the changing, shifting scenes of your life stands Christ, the Silent Commander. He knows when to say, "Foward, march!" "Stand still and see the salvation of the Lord" or "Pitch your tents for the night."

Lastly, It Will Be the Beautiful City because Jesus is there. Wherever you find Jesus, you will find heaven. His presence makes heaven.

> "I shall know Him, I shall know Him,
>   And redeemed by His side I shall stand;
> I shall know Him, I shall know Him
>   By the print of the nails in His hand."

No wonder when the little girl was dying and her mother was telling her all about heaven, about Jesus, the best and kindest man who ever lived, she exclaimed, "O Mother, if it's like that, take me there." A heaven without Jesus would be like a night without stars, at day without a sun, and a rainbow without colors. No wonder we sing:

> "O that with yonder sacred throng
> We at His feet may fall!
> We'll join the everlasting song,
> And crown Him Lord of all."

The martyrs, prophets, angels, saints, and loved ones are all waiting at the portals ready to shout, "Open wide the gates and let the redeemed of the Lord come in!" Soon it will not be "Goodnight" but "Good morning"; not "Farewell" but a thousand "Welcome home" —home with the angels, home with the saints, home with one another, and home with Jesus in that beautiful city of God in the land of endless delights.

YOUR VERDICT—FOR OR AGAINST CHRIST

What shall I do then with Jesus which is called Christ?
—MATTHEW 27:22.

Voltaire said on one occasion, in a bombastic manner, that Christ would be forgotten in less than half a century, and more theaters than churches would be built in that time. What a poor prophet he and all his colleagues since turned out to be! Infidelity has been a blind leader leading the blind. Zoroaster, the traditional founder of the religion of Persia, came along with his millions of worshipers, but today he is the relic of a bygone age. Vast throngs five thousand years ago gathered on the banks of the Nile and had their gods, temples, and altars, but today they are as dead as old King Tut. Some, even in this day, say the time will come when we will regard Jesus as we regard Aristotle, Josephus, and Confucius: wonderful men for the day in which they lived, but we have outgrown them. Will we hear of Jesus only through some undeciphered hieroglyphic? Some are saying Christianity will be supplanted by other religions; that Pilate's Man and King soon will no longer sway the multitudes. Some are saying paganism or some other form of heathenism will be the new religion. But that can never be, for they have been tried and found wanting. Found wanting because they were religious for certain classes and not for all mankind; found wanting because of the ignorance and poverty and intolerance they produced by their teachings; found wanting because they depended upon human resources. As faulty as some of these religions were, they were better than none at all. Christianity would preserve the good in all and destroy the bad.

Many are saying with Russia and others that science will be the future cure-all; that factories and railroads and industries will take the place of the church; that the radio will be used in place of prayer. Science has assorted the rocks, tunneled the mountains; made the sea a mighty highway, the sun a fuel box, turned night into day, created wholesome foods from poisons; made the nations of the earth our back-door neighbors, and made the lightnings write our thoughts. But what a mess it has made of soul virtues and spiritual ideals! Science has fought the bloodiest wars of history. Its children are liquid fire, poison gas, submarines, tear bombs, bombing planes, atomic bombs, staggering taxation, war debts and, finally, a world seething with hatred.

Some are going so far as to propose philosophy for Christianity. But this world can never be saved by the cold hand and the dead heart of philosophy. Too often its syllogisms, courts of appeal, intangible principles, vague abstractions, and rhetorical vaporings are mere wordy platitudes. Philosophy is wrong in saying that the human race is self-regenerative. Such are the force, friction, and dynamic power of sin as to prevent humanity regenerating itself.

Others are saying education and culture will save us. An education that is not bottomed on Christ is the deadliest rot this side the gates of hell. The crimes of the educated shock us. France has her universities, and yet this nation became a leading nation for infidels. It was an educated class that ordered Christ crucified. It was the educated who brought in the thumbscrew and rays of the Inquisition. An ignorant Negro preacher in Virginia declared that his race didn't have sense enough to explain away the Scriptures.

All these religious systems have failed to produce, to satisfy, and to bring about results, and the souls of men are still crying out for the living God. Jesus has never failed. He stands by all earth's great discoveries, whether they be scientific, geographic, or moral. Today all catch up Pilate's declaration and say, "Behold the Man," "Behold the King." Christ has outlived all others. Brahma hasn't any throne, the harp of Orpheus never plays, the thunders of Jupiter have died out, Egyptian mummies still sleep on, the fires of the Persians will not rekindle, and the wandering Arab finds that Mecca will not answer. But, as one has so eloquently said, "the achievements of genius, painter's brush, artist's chisel, author's pen, galleries of art from Florence to Washington, have all been busy through the ages depicting the world's thoughts of Christ."

Christ will yet stay the red hand of war and make it a fit inscription only for the denizens of hell. He will yet tame the German bear, lift Russia from gloom to gleam, dry Italy's tears, wreath with love the cold, dark brow of Spain, and finally cross the Atlantic and Pacific and become the brightest star on the horizon.

What, then, shall I do with these facts—this monumental testimony? What then, shall I do with Jesus? It's a question that you alone can answer. No priest, preacher, church, godfather, or godmother can answer for you. It's not the preacher, the deacon, or my neighbor, but "me, O Lord." We are not to be saved in masses but individually. The divine flaming interrogation must be answered by every soul on earth. We cannot transfer our responsibility nor seek refuge in substitution. You can't ward it off, dodge it, bribe it, nor escape the resounding question, "What shall I do with Jesus?"

Let the trial start! Convene the court and introduce the witness. This will differ from any other court, for all are judges and all are on the jury. There can be no change of venue, no continuation, no turning state's evidence, no mistrial, no sealed verdict, no appeal, and no retrial. I dare anyone to be listless and prejudicial. All must weigh the evidence when the life of Christ hangs in the balance and the faith and hope of countless millions are at stake. All that I ask is that you be fair and impartial. Jesus is time's greatest miracle, and there are three aspects to that miracle.

FIRST. *Look at His Early Life and Environment.* —"Can any good come out of Nazareth?" Born of a virgin in a stable! In infancy he startled a king; in childhood he puzzled the doctors; in manhood he ruled the course of nature, walked upon the billows as if pavements, and hushed the sea to sleep. He healed the multitudes without medicine and made no charge for his service. He never wrote a book, yet all the libraries of the country could not hold the books that have been written about him.

"He never wrote a song, yet he has furnished the theme for more songs than all the song writers combined. He never founded a college, but all the schools put together cannot boast of having as many students. He never marshaled an army, nor drafted a soldier, nor fired a gun, and yet no leader ever had more volunteers who have, under his orders, made more rebels stack arms and surrender without a shot being fired." The names of the past proud statesmen of Greece and Rome have come and gone, but the name of this Man abounds more and more. Though time has spread nineteen hundred years between the people of this generation and the scene of his crucifiction, yet he still lives. Herod could not kill him, Satan could not seduce him, death could not destroy him, and the grave could not hold him.

His associates were despised Gallileans, his friends publicans, sinners, blind Bartimaeuses, Mary Magdalenes, and the humbly devoted. His greatest disciple was a man who wore camel's hair and ate locusts and wild honey. His greatest preacher was an ignorant fisherman, and his greatest believer was the dying thief; yet out of this squalor, poverty, and wretchedness comes the Lion of the Tribe of Judah, the One who shall direct the stars in their courses, the "King of kings and Lord of lords."

SECOND. *No One Offered His Followers as Little as Did Jesus.* "Foxes have holes, and the birds of the air have their nests; but the Son of man hath not where to lay his head." He said in effect, "I can only offer you persecution, affliction, desertion, and sometimes even death." Who wants that? Who is willing to exchange the mansion for the desert? Who will exchange the cup of pleasure for the cup of wormwood? Had it been a matter of ceremonies, duties, formalities, and rituals, I could have understood it, yet notwithstanding its crosses, sufferings, hardships, millions more follow him than follow the glory and wealth of any conquering world hero.

THIRD. *His Death Was His Goal.* Death as a rule is kind to only a few. Except for his ignominious death, Christ would not be remembered any more that a passing Alexander the Great, or a brutal Julius Caesar. If there ever was an hour, speaking after the manner of men, when unbelief was justified, it was when Christ died. He prayed for help, but the sun in the heavens and even God himself seemed to have forsaken him. He prayed, and not an angel came to his rescue. He died as helpless as the thieves on either side. If you had been there, would you not have cried out with the others, "Come down from that cross and we will believe"? Could this be Ezekiel's rising Star, Isaiah's slain Lamb, or John's King of kings? And yet, out of the darkness, desertion, betrayal, treachery, and ignominy there is born the world's Bright and Morning Star, the Mount of Transfiguration, and the Light of the world. I ask again, what will you do with Jesus? You must do something with him. You can't delay him, shelve him, or evade him. The trial will start, and it will be brief.

Let Christ, the defendant, testify. He has always been willing to step out in open court and be examined and cross-examined. Permit me to ask Christ two questions which have been asked many times by all mankind.

FIRST. *What Do You Claim for Yourself, Any More Than Washington, Lincoln, or Lee Might Claim for Themselves?* Hear him say, "I am the vine," "I am the bread of life," "I am the truth, the way, and the life." Imagine any human being saying things like that! If not true, what blasphemy, what insane presumption, if spoken by a mere man!

SECOND. *What Do You Possess Any More Than Other Good Men Possess?* Again hear him reply, "I and the Father are one," "He that hath seen me hath seen the Father." Hear it modernists, hear it rationalists, hear it Unitarians and humanists! He allowed men to worship him, pray to him, and sacrifice to him as God, without a protest on his part. The only man besides Christ who ever allowed men to call him God was Herod; and the worms devoured him. Every incommunicable attribute of the Almighty—Omnipotence, Omniscience, Omnipresence, and Self-existence, Christ claimed to the fullest extent. How could any man possess an incommunicable attribute? He would be a God if he did.

Let us examine the witnesses, men of unimpeachable character. Hear David—he wrote the songs we will sing in the "service on high." He says, "I heard the voice of the Father say, 'This day have I begotten thee.'" God declares, "So many as the stars of the sky [in multitude] so many children shall he have, and through his name shall all families of the earth be blessed." Isaiah shouts out his divine soliloquy, "Unto us a child is born, . . . a son is given: and the government shall be upon his shoulders: . . . The mighty God, the everlasting Father, the Prince of Peace." Now hear John the Baptist, the Billy Sunday of all the disciples—the only man who ever made Herod bite the dust—who aired the hides of the Pharisees, "Behold the Lamb of God, which taketh away the sin of the world." Here comes Daniel, minister extraordinary of Babylon—a man to whom kings had no crowns nor queens any thrones. The whole world knew he could not be bought or swayed in any way. His testimony rings out like a silver bell: "Lo, I see four men loose, walking in the midst of the fire, . . . and the form of the fourth is like the Son of God." But look, here is Simon Peter, the Teddy Roosevelt of the disciples, and he says, "Thou art the Christ, the Son of the living God." Talk about your sprinters—Andrew says, "I ran and told my brother I had found the Christ." Of Nathanael, Jesus said, "An Israelite . . . in whom is no guile!" Make way for the woman of Samaria. Society, the world, and even the church would not forgive, but she goes to the city and cries to all, "Come out to the well and see a Man who told me of all the sins which I had been guilty of. Is he not the Christ?" Listen to the man born blind—all the infidels of earth cannot answer his declaration, "I once was blind but now I see."

I might call in the evangelists—John, "In the beginning God"; Matthew, "Immanuel"; Mark, "I wrote the beginning of the gospel of the Son of God." And now Thomas is ready—"Thomas, you missed a great deal by not being at prayer meeting Wednesday night. Come and thrust your hand into his side and feel the print of the nails in his hand." Poor Thomas piteously says, "My Lord and my God."

Then here is an old saint about to render his final report, and he closes his ministry with the words "Blessed be God, the Father of our Lord and Saviour Jesus Christ." Listen to Nicodemus, the greatest of all lawyers. You can't stampede him or sweep him off his feet with the sophistries of men. He declares, "Rabbi, Thou art a teacher from God."

Hear his enemies—their testimony should be considered. They cannot expect any relief by turning state's evidence. Hear Pilate—the man who lowered his colors to the crowd, who hadn't any sand in his craw, who cracked under the strain, who showed the yellow streak—hear him declare, "I find no fault in this man." Judas speaks. We will never pronounce that name without a hiss upon our tongues. The world will never forget him, because he kissed away the life of our Lord. He would have been more of a man had he spat in his face or smote him with the palm of his hand, but he kissed away the life of the best Friend the world ever had. No wonder he heard the tramp of millions climbing up the steps of time denouncing him with thunderous voices, "You're a traitor!" He saw it written in letters of fire on the walls of hell, "You're a traitor!" He heard in the jingle of silver as it fell to the ground, "You're a traitor!" What else could he do but say, "I have betrayed innocent blood" and strangle out his own existence.

I Want to Draw a Line Between the Friends of Jesus and the Foes of Jesus. In the thirty-second chapter of Deuteronomy there is a verse which all Christians lean upon, "Their rock is not as our Rock, even our enemies themselves being judges." If I could prove that not a Christian leader of note ever recanted, and every infidel or atheist of note did recant, could you follow an old hag like that? Some say Archbishop Cranmer recanted. He did, but he returned to the Lord and was burned at the stake for coming back to Christ; so finally and eventually no real Christian ever recants.

Look at the Cohorts of Infidelity. It is reported that Tom Paine said before he died: "Doctor, I'm going to hell, and you are going with me; Oh, that I could see my books burning in the flames as my poor soul shall soon burn." Renan: "O God, if there be a God, hell would be a refuge from Thy presence." Hume: I do not know his dying words, but his nurse said he died screaming, moaning, cursing, and praying, and said, "I pray God that I may never see another infidel die." Ethan Allen: Just before he passed away his little girl came to him and said, "Daddy, you say there is no God, and mother says there is one. Who must I believe?" He answered, "My child, take your mother's advice." Queen Elizabeth died praying, "My kingdom, my kingdom for one hour of prayer." Bob Ingersoll, that hired defamer of the Christian's God, who preached his gospel of filth and suicide, when delivering his brother's funeral eulogy, said, "In the night of death, hope sees a star, and listening love can hear the rustle of a wing."

Look at the Saints of Christianity. John Wesley, founder of Methodism, shouts as he passes over the river: "The best of all, God is with us." Calvin, founder of Presbyterianism: "Lord Jesus, Thou hast loved me to the end." Gladstone: "A rock in a weary land." Stonewall Jackson: "Let us pass over the river and rest under the shade of the tree." William McKinley: "Nearer, My God, to Thee, Nearer to Thee." Thomas Edison, looking out of his window, said to his doctor: "It's very beautiful over yonder." Dr. William Harper: "Now I lay me down to sleep, I pray the Lord my soul to keep." General Foch, Commanding General of the Allied armies of World War I, "Doctor, all I need now is heaven." Sainted mother, just before she entered the fields of Elysium, sang so sweetly, "Jesus paid it all."

You must account for the Gallilean. "What shall I do with Jesus?" is the question of the ages. I can account for Socrates, Plato, Cicero, and Newton, but how can you account for Jesus, the carpenter's Son, the Man who had not where to lay his head?

"But," says the infidel, "who knows who wrote Matthew, Mark, Luke, and John?" I answer, "Mr. Infidel, who knows who wrote Josephus, Shakespeare, or *Paradise Lost?*" He says, "We know certain men wrote these books because we accept the voice of tradition, testimony, and history." Again I reply, "Mr. Infidel, following the same line of reasoning, I know that Matthew, Mark, Luke, and John wrote the Gospels because I, too, accept the voice of tradition, testimony, and history. Only my testimony is ten thousand times more voluminous and has been subjected to a million times greater test and duration." Jesus has come out of the hot scorching flames of criticism without the smell of fire upon his garments. As has been said, "He is the anvil that has worn out all the hammers of opposition." Even the infidel unconsciously pays tribute to Jesus when he starts his letter—"In the Year of Our Lord." Not a wind blows upon our shores that does not come from some land which has felt the touch of his infinite hand. Scribe, Pharisee, and all would gather their freshest laurels to adorn the brow once covered with thorns. Soon all the world will be humanized and clothed in its right mind, and the earth shall be full of the knowledge of God as the waters cover the sea. Christianity is not a religion of mere revelation. Spiritualism, Eddyism, Russelism, and theosophy are all religions of revelation, but Christianity is a religion of redemption, offering salvation and eternal life through a divine, living Saviour.

Jesus stands alone. Rome had her Forum, Athens her Acropolis, Jerusalem her Temple; England has her Oxford, America her Harvard, Princeton, and Yale; and yet we have never produced another Jesus. Why?— because it would take a Jesus to forge Jesus. You can't palm off on a dying world a Jesus. If Jesus was a myth, the myth would be as great a miracle as the reality. You cannot build a temple like Christianity, with millions of flowers, on a myth. A man came to Napoleon and said, "I could invent as good a religion as Jesus did, but I could not get anyone to believe in it." "Ah," said Napoleon, "invent your religion, die for it, be buried for it, and on the third day arise from the dead, and you will have no trouble getting people to believe in it." What is the difference between Jesus and every good man who ever lived? If George Washington or Abraham Lincoln were living and were to walk down the aisle of the church, we would all stand with heads uncovered; but if Jesus were living in the flesh and should walk down the church aisle, we would all fall on our knees and sing, "Bring forth the royal diadem, and crown Him Lord of all."

After thirty-six years in the ministry, I want to say that the preaching of this Christ and his cross will move, thrill, and draw long after the fireworks of pulpit oratory have exploded and the tar barrel of the sensationalist

has ended in smoke. Who can add one embellishment
to the gospel? Yet there are those, even some ministers,
who would knock the cross from under the world and
substitute a reed of ethical culture. All of our philos-
ophies, theories, doctrines, to endure, must be lighted
from the cross.

We Must Account for Jesus. You can't confine him,
for he overleaps the boundaries of earth and time. You
can't localize him, for he belongs to every man. You
can't bury him, for he was born not to die. You can't
compromise him, for he is either all or none.

It is time for your verdict. The evidence is in. Is
it Jesus or Barabbas? Is it Jesus or self? Is it Jesus or
mammon? Is it Jesus or the world? Will the verdict
be, "Some other time," "Not tonight," "A more conven-
ient season," or will it be, "Come into my heart, Lord
Jesus," to abide and reign? Better for you never to
have been born than to decide against Jesus. Try to
compromise him, put him off, flirt with his promises,
maliciously reject him and soon, only too soon, you
will stand before the Great White Throne, and the question then will be, "What will Jesus do with me?"